KNOW
SEEK
*The Study of
the Character of
God*
WORSHIP

DAVID B. VIRTS

BLUEPRINT PRESS
INTERNATIONALE

ISBN
978-1-959365-19-8 (Paperback)
978-1-959365-20-4 (eBook)
978-1-959365-18-1 (Hardcover)

Dedication

This book is dedicated to my Lord Jesus Christ, to whom I owe everything.

Acknowledgments

I would like to thank my wife, Shirley, for her encouragement and help getting this book written and patiently teaching me much about the computer (I also got computer help from my daughter, Katrina). Also, I would like to thank my former pastor, Paul Meyer, and my current teacher, Terry Frala for going over the book theologically and helping me smooth out the rough spots.

Table of Contents

Preface

One day as this author was meditating and praying a thought from God came to him: "Do you know as much about God as you should? Or, would you like to know much more about God?" I had heard and studied a lot about God throughout the years, but I did need to know Him much better.

Thoughts like that became the genesis of the idea to do a study on the character of God from the attributes, character qualities, and word descriptions used in the Scriptures about God. I started by going to "The New Nave's Topical Bible" and began looking up the various words that were used to describe God throughout the Scriptures. Then I began to think of a title for the book when these thoughts came to me: #1, it is first necessary to come to *know* God: this happens when a person is born again, saved, converted, or experiences salvation (or one of the other descriptions of the 20+ things that happen to a person at salvation); #2, then, once a person comes to know God, it is the desire of his heart to *seek* God and to know Him far better; and, finally, #3, it is then that the person can *worship* God as Jesus said, "in Spirit and in truth." And thus this book came into being to educate people what the Scriptures say about God, and to motivate them to end up worshipping Him.

Introduction

Every serious student of the Bible has some study helps that have been developed down through the years by Bible Scholars. We do—in this day and age—stand on the shoulders of giants who have spent years studying the Scriptures and chronicling what they have learned and pass it down to us.

In this study I used "The New Nave's Topical Bible" as my primary reference. I first copied down all the references listed (and, in some cases, used cross references) to get as complete a list as possible of each attribute, character quality of God, or word description of Him. Over 50 words were chronicled from which we get a good picture of God from our perspective here on earth.

To complete the study, the author first carefully wrote down each verse; then a personal paraphrase of the verse was written to try to capture what the original author was communicating; next a two word summary (called a "handle") was written for each verse; and finally, a prayer of worship to God was recorded.

Finally, a series of questions were asked: #1, what other character qualities of God are listed together, and why are they listed together? #2, how does each character quality of God touch the life of believers? #3, and how can the believer, through each character quality, come to *know, seek, and worship* God more fully?

Prologue

Genesis 1:1: "In the beginning God . . ."

Isaiah 40:26: "Lift up your eyes on high and see: who created these? He who brings out their host by number, calling them all by name; by the greatness of his might and because he is strong in power, not one is missing."

Know

Why a book on the character of God?

Throughout the Bible every major Bible character and each writer passed on to us what they knew and had learned about the God they worshipped. Many met with God, heard His voice speaking from heaven, and some were taken up in the spirit and in visions and dreams and "saw God." Each passed on to us a wealth of information about the God we can't see yet we worship.

The key thing is this: one could describe God in hundreds of thousands of words and barely get started describing Him, but God has chosen to describe Himself to us in more than fifty different "word descriptions" (or character qualities) passed on to us in a collection of writings we now call the Bible. In it God has chosen to reveal Himself to us primarily using a series of those word descriptions. These word pictures tell us a little more about the God we serve. Each word is full of meaning; each is incomplete in itself, but each word helps describe to us a little more about our great God. To complete the picture, two thousand years ago God came to earth in the person of Jesus Christ and called Him "the Word." So to get a clearer picture of who God is, we can and must look intently at the person and life of Jesus Christ, and in doing so much about God is clarified and amplified. Until we see Him face-to-face, word pictures reveal some of God's magnificence, glory, splendor, awesomeness, and greatness. As we look intently at these word pictures and the person of Jesus Christ, we see and know God better.

Since this is the way God chose to unveil Himself to men, we must look at each word description of God, as our forefathers through the centuries have done. They searched for more and more meaning and understanding about who He is, what He is like, and especially how He chose to reveal Himself to man. Many books have been written trying to describe God by looking through those words He left behind for us to ponder. As the church age nears its end, many people have had a growing desire to search the Scriptures and discover more about God. When this era is over, and when our lives are over, we will enter His presence to worship Him as He unveils Himself to us, and this unveiling of Himself will last for all of eternity. Could it be that the church senses its time on earth is nearly over and that we are tuning up for the great "forever concert" of worshipping the God we have come to love and worship?

One day as I was thinking and praying, a question came to me from God: "Do you know much about Me, or do you just *think* you know Me well? Wouldn't you like to get to know Me better?" I then set out on a mission to know Him better and to bridge the gap between the infinite God and the fact that I am finite. I realized that many people think the way to know God better is to look at nature and the world He has made. That is a good place to start, and in Psalm 19 we are told that God's voice is booming down to us through the universe around us, beckoning us to "look up" and know Him. But, as we study science and nature, we still come up far short. We can determine that God is powerful, creative, and full of wisdom and understanding far beyond human comprehension. This is a good place to start, but it falls short of giving us an idea of the vastness of who God has revealed Himself to be.

Being a student of the Bible, I knew it introduces God to us as the "Word" (John 1:1). It further tells us that "the universe was created by the word of God", Hebrews 11:3. This explains that God spoke this world into existence! Not only is that a powerful force, one that totally escapes man, but it also gives us a clue as to how we can know Him. God has chosen to reveal Himself to man in depth and detail using words. Many times in the Bible (and especially in the Old Testament), it says, "And the LORD said . . ." or, "Thus saith the LORD . . ." The greatest outpouring of information about God—especially as He intended to communicate to man—is through the Word, which John in his Gospel identifies to us as Jesus Christ Himself. Hebrews 1 tells us that God spoke in time past through the prophets but now "in these last days has spoken unto us by his Son." The point here is this: God has chosen to use words primarily to reveal to man much about Himself, so we will look at a number of words that define and explain to us a little more about the awesome God we serve.

When God put the challenge before me, I began to use topical Bibles and concordances and looked up all the words I could find in the Bible that described each character quality of God. I listed the reference for each word. Many words and thoughts about God are duplicated many times, but each one emphasizes a little more about God and His character. For example, when doing this Bible study, a student would look up the word *love* or *power* or *knowledge* of God in a concordance or reference book and find all the verses in the Bible that use that particular word (I mainly used *Nave's Topical Bible*, but *Wilmington's Book of Bible Lists* would also be helpful). After compiling a list of the references, the student would take each verse and do a brief study on it.

Here is a sample of how it can be done: let's take for example God's power. In the charts at the end of this book is a list of many of the verses used to find out information about God's power. One of the verses is Isaiah 40:26. This first thing to do is write out the verse. Here is the verse rewritten in paraphrase form: "Lift up your eyes on high and see: who created these? He who brings out their host by number, calling them all by name; by the greatness of his might and because he is strong in power, not one is missing."

Next, paraphrase the verse. In a paraphrase you need to do several things: first, rewrite the verse in your own words. Develop your own style of writing. If you are good at writing in rhythm or in verses of poetry, use that. Second, try to get all of the content of the verse included in the paraphrase, and whenever it is possible, put the words in the first person. The words *I, me,* and *my* make the verse personal to the writer.

Here is a paraphrase of this verse: "Look up far above everything in this world and see the God who created all of these things. He has each of the stars in His creation counted—and He calls each by name! He does this because He has unlimited power and ability. He knows where each one is, and not one of them is missing."

Next, look carefully at the verse; do you notice any other character quality of God mentioned? Here God's infinite knowledge (known as His omniscience) is brought alongside His power. The verse goes on to call it "the greatness of His might and the strength of His power." This again emphasizes how much power God has. It is not adequately described simply as power; it uses a number of words to demonstrate how much power He has. Also notice that His power is called "great." Writers of Scripture struggled to express to us how powerful God is, so they often used the words "great power." We today would say His power is immense or massive. His power is far beyond our comprehension.

In the paraphrase, one has to look at the "who, what, when, why, and where" of each verse and discover its meaning and content, and as you rewrite it, let it become yours. The next thing in your study is to give each verse a one- or two-word "handle." The handle encapsulates the content of the verse and makes it easier to memorize and keep in mind for future use.

Finally, write out a prayer of application for the verse. Make the prayer personal as you pour out to God what you have discovered from the verse. When you are done with that, then the ultimate suggestion is to meditate on the verse. Take five or ten minutes to "chew the verse over in your mind" (which is a description of how to "meditate"). When you meditate on a verse or passage of Scripture, you are firmly putting it in your mind, which makes it easier to memorize.

Here are several other things to look for in the study: discover examples of His power in the various stories of the Bible; look for word pictures of His power in action (such as the east wind blowing and parting the Red Sea for the Israelites and drying it up so they could pass over); look up definitions of words you don't understand; ask questions about each verse—for example: why did the writer say it that way, or what did he mean by that phrase?

After looking up all the verses on a given character quality, write a summary. After God laid it on my heart to complete the study, I spent fifteen and a half years going over the various character qualities and descriptions of God and summarizing them. In the summary one would chronicle all the other qualities of God mentioned in conjunction with the one study (in our example, power), listing the insights given by a number of verses that point to one specific truth, and make a chart of each quality and how it relates to your life personally. In our example a chart could be made up that chronicled all the things God did for His children that demonstrated His awesome power.

Here is a brief list of the tools available to all believers:

1. Jesus told us that when the Holy Spirit came and lived in each believer, one of His jobs was to "lead us into all truth" (John 16:13). So we must pause and ask Him to reveal to us the truth of the passage we are studying.

2. Learn to paraphrase and personalize the Scripture. In the paraphrase you try to express in your own words what you believe a particular verse is saying, and in the personalization, you put it in the first person—make it yours! For example: "God created me in His image—that is, in many ways He created me like Himself."

3. Let the Scriptures define each character quality. Our definitions of God's character qualities are far short of a good clear biblical definition.

4. Always pray and ask the Spirit for guidance. Make this a prayer each time you approach the Scriptures.

5. Use the many helps available, including study Bibles, maps, concordances, lexicons, cross references, Bible dictionaries, topical Bibles, etc. (Many of these are available online.)

6. Commit yourself to a set time of study each day. Make it the same time of day, if that helps your schedule, and spend twenty minutes, forty minutes, or an hour or more.

7. Each time ask God to give you a deep hunger for His Word. God's passion is to reveal Himself to us through His Word, and He will intensify that passion as you dig into it.

8. Get a notebook, or do it on a computer. There are many helps in setting up your own Bible study. Be organized. Be thorough!

9. Share what you have learned with others. Who knows, you may end up teaching others someday—maybe even your own family.

10. Yes, it does take time and commitment, but I believe there is no greater value to your time on earth than to seek the God we worship, love, adore, and we will praise forever because He is awesome!

Seek

As one goes back and forth over each verse of the Bible that refers to a particular character quality, much is gleaned about God's existence, how man came into being, how vast God is, and how we can tap into His knowledge and His power.

Each character quality of God studied brings man to the same conclusion: God is incomprehensible! Each character quality and each verse studied tell us more, but our problem is that we are finite so we can't comprehend the vastness of our God. When it is revealed to us through a sermon or through personal Bible study, it quiets and calms our hearts. For example, some people say that when we get to heaven, we will instantly know everything. While we will know and understand much more than we do now, man will never know as much as God knows about everything—then we would be God ourselves! But the fact remains that we will spend all of eternity trying to learn more and more and comprehend more and more about our great God! What a worthy goal—to learn as much as we can about Him and increasingly learn more and more right on into eternity!

Why one more book? The primary purpose of this book is to whet the appetite of believers to dig deeper into the Word for themselves and discover more and more about the God they worship. Another main purpose is to show how we have been designed to showcase one or more key character quality of God, and to do that we will discuss several character qualities and learn from the ways God described Himself to us. If the Scriptures are inexhaustible, then there is far more to discover than we can imagine. This book is a fresh approach to studying God in that it encourages men and women of God to search the Scriptures to find gold nuggets of truth. They are there, and they are buried—like a hidden treasure—and will be found only as we learn to search for them with the eagerness and urgency we would use to look for gold or silver. Proverbs 2:4–5 tell us this: "If thou seekest her as silver, and searchest for her as for hid treasures; then shalt thou understand the fear of the Lord, and find the knowledge of God." So let's dig into the Scriptures and learn to worship the God we love.

Worship

Pause to Praise and Worship: O God, even though You are infinite and we are finite, You have taken great pains to reveal Yourself in a way that draws worship from us. We desire to learn to worship You fully and are quite aware that the only way we will do it is to dig into Your Word and see for ourselves the vastness that defines who You are. Teach each of us to worship and praise You while here on earth as we prepare for eternity. Fill our hearts with praise and worship so that we will be ready at a moment's notice throughout all of eternity to fall at Your feet and worship You!

Chapter 1

Man's Basic Questions Answered

Revelation 4:11: "Worthy are you, our Lord and God, to receive glory and honor and power, for you created all things, and by your will they existed and were created."

Throughout history, man has asked many questions such as:

- Who am I?
- Why am I here on earth?
- Where did I come from?
- What is God's ultimate purpose for man?
- In essence, what is the Bible all about?
- If God is holy, why did He allow sin to exist?

These questions have plagued man for centuries. Man has tried to answer the questions apart from God's revelation in the Bible and has come up with some of the most hopeless and nonsensical answers imaginable. Their answers have caused more confusion and fail to come up with anything that is logical and acceptable—and are definitely unbiblical! So we must go to a reliable source—the Bible—to see how knowing the character of God unlocks some of the mysteries about Him and answers man's basic questions. I believe that studying His character and the words that describe to us His character will lead us into a better understanding of ourselves and the God we serve.

1

Know

The Bible starts out "In the beginning God…" and then proceeds to answer many of man's basic questions in the story of how man was created. Man was created in the image of God. Man was created to subdue and populate the earth. Man was given dominion over all the animals. One thing is certain—if we don't accept the biblical account of creation and the history of man as it has been preserved for us down through the centuries, we will never come to know God in a way that will explain life's basic questions. Let's look at some of the character traits of God and see what answers about man's origin and existence are given in the Bible.

Let's take one of the character qualities of God that begins to unlock the truth about it as it relates to the creatures that God has made to embellish that character. The character quality is God's holiness. First, let's look at other creatures God has made. In Isaiah 6:1-3, we are introduced to creatures called "seraphim," which Isaiah saw in the temple in heaven. "Isaiah 6:2-3 says, "Above him stood the seraphim. Each had six wings: with two he covered his face, and with two he covered his feet, and with two he flew. ³ And one called to another and said: 'Holy, holy, holy is the LORD of hosts; the whole earth is full of his glory!'" When we speak of the seraphim, we need to quickly note that many have said that they are angels, but nowhere in Scripture are the seraphim specifically said to be angels. It isn't a stretch at all to view them as one of many of the creations of God. How do we know that God hasn't made dozens or even thousands of other creatures that we don't know anything about here on earth? Isn't that what the Scriptures are referring to when they speak of the "hosts of heaven"? Since we and angels are the only ones we know about here on earth, we assume that all creatures in heaven are angels, but I believe that it is not the case.

The seraphim are creatures whose purpose for existence is to reflect and put the spotlight on the fact that God is holy and anyone approaching His throne must be holy. The only mention of seraphim by that name in the Bible is here in Isaiah 6. Later on in the Bible in Revelation, we find a similar description of creatures called "living creatures" or "beasts". Listen to what it says in Revelation 4:6-11: "and before the throne there was as it were a sea of glass, like crystal. And around the throne, on each side of the throne, are four living creatures, full of eyes in front and behind: [7] the first living creature like a lion, the second living creature like an ox, the third living creature with the face of a man, and the fourth living creature like an eagle in flight. [8] And the four living creatures, each of them with six wings, are full of eyes all around and within, and day and night they never cease to say, 'Holy, holy, holy, is the Lord God Almighty, who was and is and is to come!'"

John is describing the scene around the throne of Almighty God. This is the centerpiece of heaven, the center of the whole universe, the central place where God dwells—that is, the central command center of the universe. Around the throne are four creatures (called seraphim in Isaiah) whose job it is to warn anyone coming into God's throne room that they are approaching a God who is holy and who cannot and will not be tainted by sin. So they inform anyone coming into His presence to be careful what they do and say because God is holy—that is, He is righteous and completely free of sin; He is perfect, and pure, and cannot be tainted by any creatures' sin.

God created each of these creatures for one purpose—to reflect or accent His holiness. The text tells us that the whole reason for their existence is to warn those who to approach God's throne that God is holy. We also learn that that is all they do twenty-four hours a day—unceasingly declare that God is holy. This is the entire reason for their existence—that is to reflect His holiness!

Next let's look at the character of God revealed through the hosts of angels. Sometime in eternity past, God created the angels. They were created as a higher being than man, meaning that they have more capabilities than man in man's existence on earth. God created a certain number of angels—maybe millions or billions of them—and they too were created for a specific purpose. We do not know all the things that the angels do and why they were created, but the Bible does tell us some things about them. In Hebrews 1:7, it tells us that they are "spirit beings" and "messengers." This tells us that, unlike us human beings, who are primarily physical beings, they are spirit beings with much more strength than man and with the ability to move around much quicker than man, who is tied to a physical body. It also tells us in Hebrews 1:14 and 2:16 that the angels are here on earth now to come to the aid of, and to in other ways minister to, believers as they walk the earth.

Angels, then, were created to reflect at least two character qualities of God in that they are spirit beings and they are also quite powerful—at least compared to man. Psalm 103:20 tells us, "Bless the LORD, O you his angels, you mighty ones who do his word, obeying the voice of his word!"

One example of the massive power of angels is demonstrated in Mark 16:4, where we find that Jesus' tomb had been sealed by a very large stone, indicating from the word used to describe stone that it weighed between one thousand and two thousand pounds. Then in Matthew 28:2 we read, "And behold, there was a great earthquake, for an angel of the Lord descended from heaven and came and rolled back the stone and sat on it." This is quite incredible! The word used to describe how the angel removed the huge boulder (the word is a millstone weighing 1000-2000 pounds) that had been used to seal the entrance (as described by one Bible scholar) is the same word used to describe how a person would pick up a pebble and toss it out into the street. That is truly an amazing strength—far beyond man's capabilities. What man is strong enough to pick up a boulder and toss it aside?

Another example of the amazing power of angels—at least compared to man—is the description in Isaiah 37:36 of how the angel of the Lord killed 185,000 troops of the Assyrian army in one night! That too is quite an incredible task and points out how the angels have amazing strength compared to man. In that way they too reflect the awesome power of Almighty God.

When man appears on the scene in the beginning of time, angels are already there. So back in time somewhere the angels rebelled against God. They were all created as full-grown adult-type angels. That means that they do not start out as man does as a baby angel and grow up to be adult angels. So at the time of their rebellion, they all knew what they were doing when they willingly joined Satan in his rebellion against God. It seems from the Scripture narrative that at least one-third of the angels joined Satan, or Lucifer, in his rebellion. When they rebelled, they sealed forever their fate forever, and all the angels who rebelled will eventually end up in the lake of fire (Revelation 20:10).

It is fascinating that when God created the world as recorded in the first three verses of Genesis, it immediately mentions darkness and light. There is no darkness in heaven, so when darkness showed up, it was something totally new. Darkness in Scripture often refers to the rebellion of both angels and man (as when man is saved he is said to have been brought out of darkness and into His marvelous light). It would seem from Scripture that sin and rebellion is attributable only to fallen angels and to man who have rejected God and will end up in outer darkness. When man is redeemed, he immediately had begun a process of cleaning him up (called "sanctification"), and one day he will stand before God holy and pure and sinless and able to reflect the holy character of God. Now that is astounding!

What, then, is the lake of fire? It is a reflection of God's character referred to in the Bible as the "wrath of God." In the lake of fire, the fallen, or demonic, angels and men who refuse to accept God's plan for salvation will spend all of eternity in torment. This is God's way of displaying His character through the wrath that He pours out forever on them in the lake of fire and brimstone. Throughout all of eternity, if anyone wants to know what the Bible means when it says that God is a God of wrath, all they have to do is look at the lake of fire, and they will be able to see the awful consequences of sin. Revelation 20:10 describes the lake of fire like this: "and the devil who had deceived them was thrown into the lake of fire and sulfur where the beast and the false prophet were, and they will be tormented day and night forever and ever." God's wrath will be poured out forever as a permanent reminder of the character quality that the Bible refers to as God's wrath.

Two other glaring examples of God's wrath are recorded in the Bible: God judged all sinful men in the world with a worldwide flood, which in a brief time wiped out millions of people. A second glimpse of God's wrath is when Jesus died on the cross for the sins of all of mankind. God took all the sins of man and poured them out in His wrath on His Son (who alone was without sin) so that redemption could be complete. If we keep in mind these and other examples of God's wrath poured out as recorded in the Bible, we will never have to ask for all of eternity what His wrath is all about!

For a moment, let's return to and learn some more from the discussion of angelic beings. The Bible tells us in 1 Peter 1:12 that angels do not understand redemption. They greatly desire to understand how fallen man can be redeemed. In the Garden of Eden, after man had sinned against God, God came and sought to restore fellowship with man. When God confronted them with their sin, both Adam and Eve confessed their sin, and although they made excuses, they did acknowledge that they had sinned. But when God spoke to the serpent, he did not repent or acknowledge his sin. So when the angels sinned against God, their fate was immediately sealed. Angels do not confess, repent, or exercise saving faith as man does. By contrast, each man is born a sinner, and if he is ever to escape the eternal wrath of God, he must experience salvation, in other words, he must repent of his sin and accept by grace through faith the gift of salvation.

Here's how God's character can turn sadness to hope: In the book of Genesis we are told how sin came into the world through Adam and Eve. God immediately extended His love and mercy to them and introduced them to redemption with the sacrifice of a lamb. He came to them seeking fellowship, reconciliation, and intimacy. As God's plan of redemption unfolded throughout the rest of the Bible, we see God demonstrating His mercy, love, and forgiveness again and again to man. As we look at the sad story about how man sinned in the garden, it begins to look hopeless— especially when, of the first two sons Adam and Eve, one of them killed the other. But as the plan of God for the redemption of man unfolds in the Scriptures, God shows man His mercy, love, and forgiveness when dealing with man's sin. This plan finally is seen in its entirety when Jesus completed redemption on the cross. So throughout history, man has to learn love, mercy, and forgiveness. God puts a person in a family where they learn love, mercy, and forgiveness. We work with people on a job or life vocation, and again we must learn love, mercy, and forgiveness. We all live in one of the nations of the world, and again we must learn love, mercy, and forgiveness or else we would kill and devour each other.

Throughout this period of time, God has chosen to do His work on earth in calling out for Himself a people, to use the church to accomplish His final part of redemption before judgment begins. So when we get into a local body of believers and rub shoulders with them in service for Him, what do we learn? Love, mercy, and forgiveness! Again and again in this life, we, as believers, must learn these three—especially if we are to be like our Lord Jesus Christ.

When we first see believers in eternity in Revelation 4 and 5, we see them singing the song of redemption—again reflecting God's love, mercy, and forgiveness. Wow! This tells us that the primary purpose for creating man, allowing him to sin, and then redeeming him is to reflect through man forever His holiness, love, mercy and forgiveness! Through redemption God puts the spotlight on His own character and allows man to reflect it forever. Throughout all of eternity, when anyone wants to know about His love, mercy, and forgiveness, we can all raise our hand and break out into singing, proclaiming God's great redemption. When Paul embellishes the theme for us of love in 1 Corinthians 13, he ends by saying that faith and hope will fade in eternity because they have been fulfilled, but love will remain. Is there any other character quality of God that means more to redeemed man than His great love? This is the theme of our songs forever. The angels don't understand this, nor does any other creature that God has created—only man.

Could it be, therefore, that the only purpose for which man was created is to reflect these qualities to all the rest of creation? Could it be that in each creation of God, each one or each part of His creation is there specifically to reflect one or more of God's character traits? Could it be that every creature in the universe, and all that are yet to be created throughout eternity, will each reflect another character quality of Almighty God? What an awesome thought! And this reflection of His character is the primary way we will praise and worship Him forever. We know how to worship and praise Him for His love and mercy because we have been redeemed, and that praise and worship explains to other creatures who haven't experienced His love and mercy more of His great character.

Seek

So we see so far that:

- God's creation reflects His power, wisdom, and understanding.
- Angels were created to show God's power (even to man) and to reflect the fact that God is a spirit being.
- The lake of fire was made to show to the entire universe throughout all of time that God is a God of wrath.
- Man was created to put the spotlight on God's love, mercy, and forgiveness.
- And the seraphim around the throne along with the angels will both help man accent and point to the holiness of our God.

God is a creative God with unlimited possibilities and unlimited designs and plans for each creation. Could it be that He created, or has been creating, many different creatures or parts of His entire creation, each one with the plan in mind to reflect another of His character qualities? Scholars have identified more than fifty different traits or characteristics of God in the Scriptures. These may be limited to man's finite understanding of an infinite God. God may be able to be described Himself in hundreds or thousands or more ways, and God, being the Great Creator, may find it appropriate to identify Himself, or unveil Himself, in yet many more ways to all of His vast creation! Imagine throughout all of eternity getting to know more and more about an infinite God as He unveils to the universe an infinite rainbow of His character qualities that will dazzle each creature! Wow!

In every glimpse we have of man in eternity, we will be joining all of God's creatures in singing praise to Him. Each time in eternity we see redeemed man, we see and hear them singing the praises of God, especially those songs about their redemption. Won't that be astounding? Throughout the rest of our existence, as we serve the King of kings and the Lord of lords, we will have the priceless privilege of proclaiming God's love, mercy, and forgiveness—because we alone have been redeemed! What a great way to spend eternity serving God and our Lord Jesus Christ!

Worship

Pause to Praise and Worship: O God, what an awesome God You are! We are in awe of the plan You have for us and are greatly humbled by the challenge to us to reflect Your holy character, and Your love, mercy, and forgiveness. Teach us daily to learn these basic skills so that we can in eternity burst forth many times with expressions of our gratitude and praise because You have set Your love and mercy on us—totally undeserving sinners who have been saved by Your grace. We stand in awe of You.

Chapter 2

Why Study God?

Acts 17:28: "For in him we live, and move, and have our being."

- Who is God?
- Why can't we see Him?
- If we could see Him, what would He look like?
- How can we come to know a God we can't see?
- How can we come to know Someone who is impossible to comprehend?
- Where is He?
- How far away is heaven?

These and many other questions have plagued man for years. Is God unknowable? No! In fact, God has taken great pains to reveal Himself to man throughout the centuries. At first God walked through the garden to have fellowship with Adam and Eve and spoke directly to them. Then, after man sinned and turned his back on God, God immediately came down to talk with him again and sought to restore fellowship. From that time on and throughout the centuries, God has revealed Himself to man in many different ways.

Know

Do we wait for God to reveal Himself to us in a dream or vision? God did reveal Himself to man many times in the Scriptures, in person, through dreams, and through the prophets of old; but now the primary way He seeks to be known to us is through His Word—and using words! Visions, dreams, and prophecies were a significant part of God's speaking to mankind—especially in Old Testament times (see Hebrews 1:1–2). In the few glimpses of God that man has had with their physical eyes, the descriptions of Him that the person who saw Him tried to give leave a lot to the imagination and are woefully inadequate to describe what that person actually saw. So, where does that leave us today, thousands of years later? Where does one start in coming to know such a holy, awesome, and majestic God?

The first and most basic thing we must recognize about God is that He is a Spirit (John 4:24). You cannot see a spirit, so if you are looking with physical eyes for One who is unseen, you will be extremely limited in what you will ever know about God. The second thing we must face is that man is now primarily a physical being. So for us to come to know God, who is Spirit, we must use spiritual eyes. The problem? We are born into this world spiritually dead, and until we are "born again," as Jesus said to Nicodemus in John 3, we "cannot see the kingdom of God," and more specifically, we cannot come to know God. But when we are born again, God's Spirit begins to illuminate our minds so that we can begin to understand all that our finite minds can comprehend about the infinite God. This first step is essential to knowing God so one can begin to seek Him and worship Him.

As we look at the Word of God, how do we come to know God? One of the ways to begin is to look at the many words that are used to describe Him, words such as *love, power, omniscience, omnipotence, wisdom, mercy, understanding, incomprehensible, unchangeable,* and so on. Then, as we see how these character qualities are defined and interrelated, we can begin to come to know the God of the Bible. Also, we can look at the examples of each quality as it is found in the Bible. Each character quality discovered in Scripture is a window through which man can look in and get a small glimpse of the greatness of our God. The two *big* picture windows from man's viewpoint are God's love and His mercy combined with His forgiveness. These two qualities give us the clearest picture of the heart of God for us and become the dearest qualities to a spiritually reborn sinner.

One of the oldest books of the Bible is the book of Job. The example of Job's life teaches us much about suffering and pain and how Job handled it with patience. When you look at the first several chapters of the book, you notice a dialogue between God and Satan as it relates to the trials that were just about to come on Job. The question that begs to be asked is: How did Job know about the discussion between God and Satan that had taken place? Was it before he was hit broadside with his trials? As you read further in the book, you discover that Job knew God pretty well, but God broadened his understanding of Himself by speaking directly to Job. He asked Job where he was when He—God—created the earth, set the bounds for the oceans and the height of the hills, created the leviathan, and so on. So God revealed it to him after his trials and after he had come to know Him much better. Then Job understood the great conflict of the ages between God and satanic forces.

After Job had a long lecture from God about Himself in chapters 38–41, Job was so overwhelmed by his encounter with Almighty God that he said in 42:6, "therefore I despise myself, and repent in dust and ashes." (see also verses 2–6). When Job heard from God and had his knowledge of Almighty God broadened, and after he had seen his own sinfulness and repented from it, *then* he understood what had happened in chapters 1 and 2 when Satan attacked him; and he saw himself as "abhorrent" and in need of constantly turning away from who he was—a sinner—and to God. We, too, can learn much about God when we learn to humble ourselves before Him, turn from our sin to Him, and then begin to study the Word and look at the character of God as it has been revealed to us. Much insight can be ours about the spirit world if we first come to know Almighty God, and when we do, it gives us added incentives to search the Scriptures diligently and allow God to reveal Himself to us.

Why should we study the character of God?

Since God has taken great pains to reveal Himself to us and has left many visible evidences of His power, His glory, His majesty, and His infinite wisdom and understanding, our curiosity about Him is intensified. Our challenge is to take that basic curiosity about God, and, for those of us who are redeemed and have God's Spirit living in us, allow Him to reveal to us a wealth of insight about our great God.

We read in the Scriptures that God is holy, light, love, or just, and each of these words gives us a further word picture of God and more insight into who He is and what He is like. For example, we read in 1 John 4:8 that God is love, and then throughout the Bible God lays out illustration after illustration of how He loved individuals, His children, His people, etc.

One of the incredibly fascinating things about His love is that love cannot be fully defined unless and until it is clearly understood and defined from the character of God Himself (and this is true of each word description of God). Man defines love in many ways—for example: "If you love me, then I will love you." Or man defines love as a feeling, which can change or go away at times. But when we see God's love, He started out choosing to love an individual or to pour out His love on a nation. God has in mind the end product of His love, that is, to call out for Himself a people or a nation on whom He has decided to pour out His love. Then ultimately His desire is to bring glory back to Himself. When you look at man's love, it is at best fickle; but when you look at the love of God, you discover that His love is permanent and not a selfish love like the love we can have for one another. God's love is a love that gives, and that love endures forever.

The conclusion we come to is this: the character qualities God says we are to copy, like love, can only be understood by a thorough examination of God and His character. He alone defines the kind of love we are to imitate.

Many might say, "But I want to come to know God through nature." A person can learn about God, His power, His majesty, His glory, and His infinite wisdom and understanding from nature. Who hasn't stood out under the stars at night and looked in awe and wonder at His creation? Or watched a sunrise or a sunset or a magnificent storm building? The Bible tells us in Romans 1 that man *can* learn about God from His universe, and Psalm 19 tells us that the heavens are like a giant boom box, telling us of His might and majesty. But if we rely only on what we can learn through nature, we will miss vast areas of knowledge. God intended us to know much more about Himself than what we can learn from nature. He has taken great pains to preserve for us His Word written down, which explains to us in great detail, in a giant word picture, much about Himself. He longs for us to know about His love, mercy, and forgiveness, which one cannot learn from nature. These can be learned only when we look at the way He showed His love to individuals and peoples throughout the ages and through the information that we have about God and His Son, Jesus Christ. The only objective information we have about God is found in the Scriptures.

Seek

We are going to spend eternity with God in heaven. We must get started somewhere in getting to know Him, and since there is such a vast amount to learn about Him, we must get started now. From the day we are born again, God puts in us a deep desire to know Him, and it is a thirst that intensifies with each year we live. The Bible is our handbook, and to begin on that eternal journey of getting to know the infinite God, we must look carefully—for now anyway—at how God has chosen to reveal Himself to us. The vast amount to learn about Him is overwhelming, but if we are to get to know this God who loves us so much, we must take our handbook and begin to know and love and adore and worship the One whose awesome character has so captured our existence. Getting to know Him precedes our worship of Him, and every bit of information we can learn about Him draws us deeper into love for Him and worship of Him.

Why study God's character? Another question can be asked: What effect on my life could I expect from studying God's character? Is there any practical value to add to my daily life by finding out more about God? Yes! A good example is when we study the power of God. When we look at the Word and begin to get a picture of what God did for His people in the past and what the Scriptures tell God can do, it boggles the mind and inspires us to put our faith and confidence completely in Him as He directs our lives and the world around us.

For example, the Bible tells us that:

- God parted the Red Sea by causing a great wind to blow all night so they went across on dry land!
- God spoke the world and the universe into existence in six days!
- The angel of the Lord killed 185,000 soldiers in a single night in King Hezekiah's day!

- In the days of Jehoshaphat, an army of one million men was wiped out without firing a shot (or lifting a sword as they did in those days), and this army was led into battle by the choir!
- God caused a woman who was a virgin to conceive and give birth!
- In time to come, when Christ returns with His saints, He will destroy His enemies with the breath of His mouth!
- A one-hundred-year-old man and his ninety-year-old wife gave birth to a healthy baby boy!
- A tiny baby that was born in a stable was actually the Creator of the universe.

These, along with hundreds of other examples from the Bible, tell us about the mighty and awesome power of God. So how does this apply to our lives today? Let's pause and ask ourselves some personal questions that plug God's power into our everyday lives:

1. If I am in a pinch today, can God do a miracle like He did in those days and bail me out?

2. When powerful satanic forces threaten to wipe me out, does Almighty God restrain them, and can He destroy their powers as He did in biblical days?

3. When God has given me an impossible-looking task, can I believe He will come through for me and help me accomplish the job?

4. If the world is set against me and has me hemmed in, can God still defeat the forces of evil that control this world system under which we live?

5. When a number of judicial decisions come down that are in defiance of God's laws and commands in His Word, can I still believe that God will take vengeance on my enemies and bring victory?

6. When I see the evil and vile forces of this world kill innocent babies by the millions, is God still in control? And can I believe that righteousness yet will prevail? And that wickedness will be put down?

7. As I look at history, I see many great revivals where scores of people repented of their sin and turned to God. Can this be repeated in my day?

To these, and many other questions like them, we can give a resounding "Yes!" The Scriptures tell us that God never changes and that Jesus Christ is the same today as He was yesterday and will always remain the same (Hebrews 13:8). God can and will—and He is able and does—intervene on our behalf at a moment's notice, just like He did for the great heroes of the Bible. If for a moment we doubt God's ability, then we know little of the power of God, as spoken of in the Scriptures. For these and many other reasons, we must search the Word and see for ourselves what God has done and what He wants to do for His children in this day and age. When the Bible says that God is able, then we must learn to act in faith on His words. When we see how God came to the rescue of His children in biblical days, we can have our faith boosted to believe that He will act on behalf of us today.

Many of man's biggest questions can, therefore, be answered from a careful study of God's character. Even questions that are some of the toughest ones to figure out have at least a partial answer (and I believe a complete answer) in the character of God.

Questions like: Since God is a holy God, since He can do anything He pleases, and since He is all powerful, then why does He allow sin to dominate in our world? Or: Why did God allow sin to exist in the first place? Or: Why is man born with a sinful nature? Doesn't that give him a distinct disadvantage in making it in this world?

This book was written to take a careful look at the Scriptures and their descriptions of God and come up with some of the answers to life's biggest questions. As we spend time combing through the Bible, looking at it with vigorous enthusiasm, and seeing what it says about Almighty God, we will have many of our questions answered and in the process greatly expand our knowledge of the One with whom we will spend eternity. It is then that we begin to bow in worship before our God.

Worship

Pause to Praise and Worship: O God, You have chosen to reveal Yourself to man, and especially to Your children. Since there is so much we don't know about You, would You reveal Yourself to me as I study the Bible with the intent of getting to know and worship You? Draw me into a close relationship with You so that my heart will become a worshipping heart and my mouth will speak often of praise and adoration to You. To that end I give myself to You.

Chapter 3

Love: Undeserved and Overwhelming

Romans 8:38–39: "For I am persuaded, that neither death, nor life, nor angels, nor principalities, nor powers, nor things present, nor things to come, nor height, nor depth, nor any other creature, shall be able to separate us from the love of God, which is in Christ Jesus our Lord."(KJV)

- What is it?
- Who gets it?
- Why is man so enthralled with God's love?
- How do I mirror God's love?
- What other character qualities of God are mentioned with God's love?
- How did God demonstrate His love to man down through the ages?
- What is the greatest demonstration of love in the Bible?
- How does God's character define love?

Of all the characteristics of God revealed to man, the one that touches man more deeply, and the one most admired by man, is God's love. Why is that? Many reasons can be given, but here are a few:

- Man is dwarfed by God, who is infinite; and to think that the Creator, the God of the universe, would take the initiative to love man is overwhelming!

- Why would God love the unlovely, the sinner, or the whole world?
- How could a holy God love men who are in rebellion against Him?
- His love, and the resulting actions, His mercy and forgiveness, are the themes of our songs throughout all of eternity!

In the Old Testament God's love and God's mercy are mentioned together a number of times. And in the same breath they are specifically referred to as "the lovingkindness of God." Also, it is difficult to explain God's mercy and love without also mentioning His infinite grace. Let's define each of these and show the difference between them, even though they are closely related.

When the Bible teaches us about God's love, it conveys the idea of Almighty God loving powerless, sinful men; our holy God deciding to love an undeserving sinner; the One who defines love stooping to love the most unlovely person. In this way the Bible describes the motivation behind redemption. Why would a holy God love and provide forgiveness for sinful man? Only infinite love could stoop to do such a thing, and in man's wildest imagination, he cannot fathom that love!

Since God decided to love man, He must help helpless man deal with his sin, rebellion, and transgression of God's standards and laws. This is where mercy comes in. What began in the heart of God, love, was extended down to man in mercy, and the power source for man to absorb God's love and mercy is found in God's grace. God had to have mercy on helpless man because man could not redeem himself, and then He gave man the power to live a holy life.

Know

It would take another book to describe all the Bible tells us about God's love (and probably all the books in the world). So here we can only summarize some of the thoughts on this enormous subject. Some of the greatest thoughts about God's love are touched on here.

God's love takes the initiative to reach down to man. The Bible tells us in Romans 3:11 that no one naturally seeks after God or understands Him. So, since no man throughout history has ever sought God, God had to take the initiative to seek man. This is His great love. Immediately after Adam and Eve sinned in the garden, God came to them—and I believe that throughout all of history every man that has ever lived God has sought to redeem, but only a few respond to His love and accept it.

God's love fills man's deepest longings. Man seeks fulfillment and satisfaction, but the temporal things in this world fall far short of complete satisfaction. When God restores His people fully, He tells us in Jeremiah 31:14, "I will feast the soul of the priests with abundance, and my people shall be satisfied with my goodness, declares the LORD." This tells us that the spiritual leaders of our people will be totally satisfied when His goodness is poured out. Our satisfaction is complete only when the love and mercy of God are poured out on us in eternity. Only then will the deepest longings and desires of man's heart find their fulfillment. Man yearns to be loved and accepted, and only God's great love can do that.

God's love is infinite. Ezekiel 16:8 brings out a good description of God's infinite love for His people. "When I passed by you again and saw you, behold, you were at the age for love, and I spread the corner of my garment over you and covered your nakedness; I made my vow to you and entered into a covenant with you, declares the Lord God, and you became mine." What a vivid description of how God's infinite love covers man's worst sins and iniquities and makes us His beloved children! This is God's love in action preparing us to move out of our sins and into His infinite love—and not only that, but again we will be reflecting that love forever.

God's love is universal; that is, it is not just exclusively for some people—His love reaches everyone. "For God so loved the world . . ." John 3:16 tells us—so God's love is reaching down to all men. First John 2:2 also tells us that Jesus didn't die just for the sins of those who were going to be saved; it says, "He is the propitiation (God's complete satisfaction) for our sins, and not for ours only but also for the sins of the whole world." This means He is the complete satisfaction before God for our sins, and not just for ours only, but also for the sins of everyone in the whole world. This tells us the breadth of God's great love reaches out to everyone!

When Jesus walked this earth, He demonstrated this further by specifically physically touching those who were sick, handicapped, and even those who had highly contagious diseases, like lepers. This is a beautiful picture of God's reaching down and touching unlovely people. Another way the breadth of His love is seen is when, in the Old Testament, He told His people to be especially kind to "the stranger, the fatherless, the widow, and the foreigner." God loves people—*all* people!

God's love also melts our worst fears. We all face fears of one kind or another, but when God draws near to us in love, His first message to us is, "Do not fear, because I am with you." This phrase is repeated over and over in the Bible; we are told hundreds of times not to fear. Fear paralyzes us, while love frees us. Because of His presence and His great love, we are freed to be bold, even in the face of the greatest danger or as we face our greatest fears.

God's love also chastens. God's special love for His children is illustrated for us constantly in Scripture in the way He loved, reached out to, blessed, and chastened His special people. Because of His love, He stays with us and keeps cleaning us up, and all because we are His specially chosen people. He implores His children to walk in His ways and keep His commandments hundreds of times so He could pour out His vast supply of blessing on them by grace. This is also referred to in the New Testament as God's conquering love reached out, not only to His special chosen people, the Jews, but also to the Gentile world and believers around the world.

God's love both chastens and disciplines His children. Every parent knows that without correction love cannot be shown. Hebrews 12:6–7 tells us, "For the Lord disciplines the one he loves, and chastises every son whom he receives." [7] It is for discipline that you have to endure. God is treating you as sons. For what son is there whom his father does not discipline?" The Lord shows His love to us by chastening us when we veer off course in life. He actually chastens harshly every person whom He will bring in as His child! So God's chastening us when we drift away from Him proves to us that He really does love us!

God's love brings us out of bondage. One of the premier examples of God's love is when Israel was in bondage in Egypt. Did God enjoy seeing them in bondage? Did He do nothing about it? Did He show mighty wonders and unfailing love when He brought them out of slavery and into the land of promise? Will He do the same for each of us because of His unfailing love? Yes!

God's love takes action to bring us into intimacy with Him and to complete the process of redemption. One of the ways God discloses to man His great love is in the way we become believers. Jesus said in John 12:32, "And I, when I am lifted up from the earth, will draw all people to myself." What He was saying was that when He is lifted up from the earth, that is, when He was crucified, He then drew all believers to Himself. So when a person comes to God in faith and is born again, he is really being drawn to the cross and to God by Jesus Christ Himself. And, in speaking of His specially chosen followers who would carry on after He was gone, He said in John 15:16, "You did not choose me, but I chose you and appointed you that you should go and bear fruit and that your fruit should abide, so that whatever you ask the Father in my name, he may give it to you." We think we chose to follow Christ, but we didn't. He chose us and set it up so that we would go forth, have a fruitful ministry, and bear permanent fruit—so much so that whatever we ask the Father in His name, He will give to us. How is that for a love that takes action? Man is first drawn to Jesus Christ in salvation and then given a task to complete. In that task that believer will then need eternal resources to accomplish it; so he is given "whatever you ask My Father in My name"! That is love that begins the process and then completes it—both now and on into eternity.

God's love conquers our feelings of being unlovely and unworthy of His love. God chooses to set His love on the unlovely and unworthy so that He can then demonstrate His power on earth through them. Man has trouble with God because he can't see Him, but if a person is looking, he can see demonstrations of God's love through His people and in many other ways. God has chosen to showcase His power at times in history, like the delivery of the Israelites out of bondage in Egypt. He showed the world amazing power over all other gods, as well as His complete control over what man wrongly terms as "the laws of nature." Why did God do that? Because He loves His people. And though they didn't seem worthy of that love, still He poured it out on them—and does the same for us today. This is how we see God's love connected with His awesome power.

God's love shows no favoritism. What does God do for the outcast or the downtrodden? Deuteronomy 10:17–18 tells us that the Lord our God is a God above all other gods and a Ruler over all the rulers of the world. He is a great, a fantastic God, who is immensely strong, He is One to be feared, and He doesn't discriminate by regarding one person above another. He also takes no bribes. But He does bring about justice for those who are without an earthly father and also for the widow. He loves foreigners and makes sure they are provided for—both in food and clothing. How is that for a God who personally takes care of the downtrodden or forgotten ones of society? His love reaches down to all of us—both the kings and rulers of this world and those who are at the bottom of the social structure.

When we see God's love in action, He is constantly forgiving our sin. Second Samuel 12:24 tells us that after King David's great sin against God with Bathsheba and after the serious consequences of that sin to King David and Bathsheba by taking the life of their first son, then King David comforted Bathsheba, his wife, and went in to her again, and she became pregnant, and gave him another son. David called the son, Solomon, and then the text adds these words: "And the Lord loved him." So, even after David's horrible sin, God forgave him and gave him another son, and God loved that son! That's love in action, constantly forgiving us when we make a mess of things.

God's love is certainly generous. Many times in the Bible we are told that God's children are His inheritance. That means those who are born again are heirs of all God has planned for them. We have a vast supply of God's riches at our disposal and will inherit a kingdom that is far beyond our imagination. Romans 8:17–18 says, "and if children, then heirs—heirs of God and fellow heirs with Christ, provided we suffer with him in order that we may also be glorified with him. [18] For I consider that the sufferings of this present time are not worth comparing with the glory that is to be revealed to us." Since we are His children, then we are His heirs to all God has and joint-heirs with Jesus Christ. Paul considered that the sufferings of this present life are not worthy to be compared with the glory that will be unveiled in us, His special chosen children. Because of His love, God is generous to us and pours out on us all that an heir to a massive kingdom would expect.

God's love "fires up" the praise of His people, and that brings praise and worship back to Him. Psalm 63:3 says, "Because thy lovingkindness *is* better than life, my lips shall praise thee."(KJV) As we walk with God and mature in our relationship with Him, we learn to praise Him more and more. This is a crescendo of praise that at times captivates us and enthralls us with His love.

One of the great contrasts in the Bible is God's love and God's wrath. We see this contrasted in Isaiah 54:7–8: " 'For a brief moment I deserted you, but with great compassion I will gather you. [8] In overflowing anger for a moment I hid my face from you, but with everlasting love I will have compassion on you,' says the LORD, your Redeemer." The LORD here is saying that it was just for a brief moment that He forsook Israel, His children; but because of His great love and mercy, He has regathered them. He showed them only a little of His wrath at that time—in fact, He hid His face from them for a just a few seconds; but then He gathered them in His great arms of love and kindness to show them mercy, and this came from the Lord, the One who bought them out of sin's slave market! What a contrast! How can anyone love and yet show wrath to the same people and at the same time? Only God can do that because His wrath didn't consume them. He waited for them to turn back to Him, and then He poured out His love on them. The same is true for us today!

God's love will shine through His children. First John 4:7-8 says, "Beloved, let us love one another, for love is from God, and whoever loves has been born of God and knows God. [8] Anyone who does not love does not know God, because God is love." He is telling us, His dear children, that we must learn to love our fellow believers. Why? Because true love comes only from God, and when we are born again, it shows that we have been loved by God because God is love. God's love is so powerful it flows right through us to other believers. This love for one another is the superglue that holds the body of Christ together, and it is really His love that holds all of us together and is making all of us into one body. His love is seen throughout all of His body. When the world gets a glimpse of Christians loving one another, it is a powerful message of how God's love can change their lives.

God's love bridges a huge chasm. Love reaches out and does whatever necessary to bridge a gap. God reached down—way down—and successfully rescued sinful creatures from the eternal ravages of hell. But He didn't stop there; He then set a plan in eternity past to redeem man, declare him just and righteous, and then put each one through a cleaning-up process (called in the Bible "sanctification"). To help with that process, God gave man the gift of eternal life, assured him of a home forever in heaven with Him, and then gave him the most amazing eternal occupation imaginable—to accent His mercy, His love, and His forgiveness forever! Wow! That makes those who are saved want to shout "Hallelujah!"

Seek

Many examples of God's great love are in the Bible, and it is here we pause to seek God. Each of these stories tells us of His immense love and how it impacted that person's life. One of the most moving stories is told during Jesus' earthly ministry about a woman simply known as Mary Magdalene. When Jesus met her, she was "demonized" by evil spirits and was a mess physically, spiritually, mentally, and emotionally. The Scriptures indicate to us that those who are "demonized" suffer immensely from these and other disorders, but Jesus had compassion on her and healed her. As we follow the steps of this woman, we find some encouraging and helpful insights: When a person is as deeply emotionally disturbed as Mary was, what would be his or her response?

Mary Magdalene's life demonstrates intimacy. It seems that some people have a deeper walk with the Lord spiritually. They seem to walk so close to Him, so much so that they "breathe His presence." Many people like that have been healed of deep emotional and mental difficulties—the same difficulties that brought them to the Lord in the first place. The Scriptures tell us that those who are forgiven much also are the ones who love much. A person doesn't have to go into deep sin to love the Lord so much, but the point is this: When people realize how much they have been forgiven, they end up with a deeper love for the Lord. They have come up against the great love of God, and that love has enveloped them to the point where they are consumed by His love. This was Mary Magdalene.

The next times we meet her are just before the cross, at the cross, and at the tomb—but the climax for her came when the Lord chose her to be the first person He revealed Himself to after He was raised from the dead. He simply asked her, "Lady, why are you weeping?" In this statement

Jesus shows the deep love of God that literally covers up and overwhelms a believer. She had been forgiven much, been healed thoroughly, and now she simply poured out her love to her dear Lord. Mary seems to be the only one who really got it that Jesus said He was going to come back to life, so she stayed by the tomb until her passion for her Lord was satisfied. This is how God's love can totally transform a person and draw them into an intimate relationship with Him—all the way to total satisfaction.

The vastness of God's love is obvious in these and other verses. It also brings us to one important fact: the love of God is demonstrated in many ways but chiefly in God's sending His Son to die for man's sin. Jesus' life, death, resurrection, and ascension are the outpouring of God's love on a sinful world. When you contrast the character of God as being holy, righteous, and just with man's sin, rebellion, and helplessness, it makes one stand in awe of God's great love. Love is not just a nice, warm, fuzzy feeling down inside a person; love must be seen in action. John 3:16 informs us that "God so loved this world that He gave . . ." One day this vast love will totally envelop us.

One closing thought about God's love is explained to us by the apostle Paul in Romans 8:31–39. Here is the powerful, indestructible love of God in action. The following are the words of these verses in a paraphrase: "Since we are being transformed into the image of God and made like Christ, what response is appropriate? If God is on our side, who could ever stand against us? Almighty God didn't even spare His own Son but allowed cruel men to crucify Him so that all of mankind could be delivered from His wrath. Since He did that for us, is there anything else He wouldn't do for us?"

Who could make a charge against God's special chosen people and make that charge stick? God is the One who declares sinful people righteous, so who can point a finger at you and condemn you? Wasn't it Christ who died for us? And more than that, who rose again breaking sin and death's power, and who right now is standing at the place of power and authority of Almighty God—interceding for believers?

- What could possibly separate us from Christ's love?
- Could the deepest trial a human being could go through?
- Could distressing life-and-death situations?

- Could those who are trying to take our lives and cut off our heads separate us from His love?
- Could famine or drought or losing all we have, including our clothes?
- Or could dangerous and treacherous circumstances?
- Or even losing our head in execution—could any of these things separate us from His great love? The Scriptures tell us that this world is hounding us and trying to execute us like an animal that is being hunted to be slaughtered!
- The answer is a resounding *NO*! In spite of these difficulties, we will end up more than conquerors because we are being held constantly by God's great love for us! I am absolutely convinced that death, life, angels, angelic beings at all levels, not any powerful force in the universe, not now or ever, nothing high or low, nor any other creature in the universe will ever be able to separate us from God's great love that was poured out on us through Jesus Christ our Lord!"

I am convinced that no other character quality of God means more to the believer than God's unfailing and immeasurable love. The greatest feeling in the world is to know that Someone loves me—far more than any other human being can. He understands me, He knows me thoroughly, and yet since He redeemed me, I know His love has overwhelmed me. Now I truly feel loved and cared for by One who is fully capable of doing it. No, nothing will ever separate me from that love!

Worship

Pause to Praise and Worship: O God, thank You so much for deciding to love me and to love the world so much that You gave Your only Son to come to earth and die for my sins so that I could live with You forever. Your love ignites my heart in worship and praise, and as we gaze into the glimpses of eternity revealed in Your Word, we will be giving ultimate praise and worship to You forever. I bask in Your love, and it fills my heart with praise and worship that will take me forever to express to You. Again, thanks for Your great love.

Chapter 4

God's Power: Massive and Available

Psalm 97:4–5: "His lightnings light up the world; the earth sees and trembles. ⁵ The mountains melt like wax before the LORD, before the Lord of all the earth."

- How powerful is God?
- What is God capable of doing with His power?
- What are biblical examples of how powerful He is?
- Is there anything He cannot do, in terms of lack of power?
- How do I see His power displayed in our world today?
- Are the "laws of nature" (as man calls them) actually evidences of God's power?
- How can I see His great power demonstrated in my life?

Man would probably say that God is very powerful, and they would stop there. Man looks at power in terms of what the person with the power can and cannot do. When they see things in our world that seem beyond the power of God to do, such as speak the word and create the universe or to put an immediate stop to all evil, they conclude that God really isn't as powerful as many say He is. Man may ask, "Is there anything that God cannot do?" The answer is this: as far as His ability is concerned, He can do anything; yet there are certain things that He *will not* do because they violate His character and His program for this world and for sinful mankind. Ability speaking, God could wipe out all evil instantaneously, or He could have never allowed sin to exist in the first place. But if He did that, then we would have no idea what righteousness and holiness are, and we would know nothing of His fierce anger against sin! So His plan to explain Himself to man is to give us a number of attributes, or character qualities, and through them He explains to finite man more and more about Himself! This is the wonder of what we will be discovering eternally. To grapple with these is to grapple with our finite minds the infinite God.

Know

To get a glimpse of the power of God—and especially in conjunction with the other attributes of God—let's look first at what the Bible says about God being a God of power.

God's power is supreme; that is, it is unmatched by all other power. Deuteronomy 3:24 gives us a comparison of God and the rest of the gods of this world. Listen to the question asked at the end of the verse: "'O Lord GOD, you have only begun to show your servant your greatness and your mighty hand. For what god is there in heaven or on earth who can do such works and mighty acts as yours?" Here Moses was recounting all the mighty acts of power that God had shown since He brought Israel out of Egypt and destroyed the kings along the east side of the Dead Sea and the Jordan River. The point is this: no other god can do these great acts of power, so God stands alone as Almighty God.

God's power is unsurpassed in the spirit world. A sobering account of the awesomeness of our God is found in Deuteronomy 32:39. Here is how it reads, "See now that I, even I, am he, and there is no god beside me; I kill and I make alive; I wound and I heal; and there is none that can deliver out of my hand." God is saying that He is the only God, and no other god is My equal. God has power to kill and power to bring back to life again. God can wound a person and heal them of that wound. And further, no one can escape from God! The contrast here between Almighty God and the puny gods of this world is breathtaking. Hebrews 2:14 tells us that the power of death is in the hands of the devil, but does the devil have the power to create life or to bring one who has died back to life? *Never!*

God's power is limitless. When Job was answering his friends, he listed a number of fantastic things God can do. In Job 9:4–12, he says, "He is wise in heart and mighty in strength—who has hardened himself against him, and succeeded?—⁵ he who removes mountains, and they know it not, when he overturns them in his anger, ⁶ who shakes the earth out of its place, and its pillars tremble; ⁷ who commands the sun, and it does not rise; who seals up the stars; ⁸ who alone stretched out the heavens and trampled the waves of the sea; ⁹ who made the Bear and Orion, the Pleiades and the chambers of the south; ¹⁰ who does great things beyond searching out, and marvelous things beyond number. ¹¹ Behold, he passes by me, and I see him not; he moves on, but I do not perceive him. ¹² Behold, he snatches away; who can turn him back? Who will say to him, 'What are you doing?'"

Not only does man have no idea what God is able to do, but he can't even enumerate all the vast things He is capable of doing! Since there is no limit to His power, we can ask Him to do anything for us—even though it seems far beyond possible to us.

God's power defies our ability to describe it. Man looks at certain things and thinks of strength and power—things like steel, titanium, atomic bombs, or nuclear energy, or even the strength of many people banded together to accomplish a certain purpose. But God measures strength in vapor or wind! Psalm 68:34-35 says, "Ascribe power to God, whose majesty is over Israel, and whose power is in the skies. ³⁵ Awesome is God from his sanctuary; the God of Israel—he is the one who gives power and strength to his people. Blessed be God!" Everything in the universe points to the strength and power of God. He proves it with His careful protection of His people Israel, but more than that in the clouds themselves! Man mistakenly calls clouds, wind, and rain "the forces of nature," but God creates these. One time while living in Nebraska, during a very wet spring, one night the weather service reported that in every reporting station in the state, there had been three-plus inches of rain. Now that's a lot of water! Someone could figure how many million gallons of water had fallen—and to think that God put it all up there in vapor and mist, and it came down in the precise place planned by God! Nahum 1:3 amplifies on this when it says, "The LORD is slow to anger and great in power, and the LORD will by no means clear the guilty. His way is in whirlwind and storm, and the clouds are the dust of his feet." God's power is seen in the variety of weather phenomenon. Job 12:15 gives a good example of the awesome power of our God: "If he withholds the waters, they dry up; if he sends them out, they overwhelm the land." Isn't it instructive to watch how He holds back the waters so that a drought comes, and at times He sends an abundance of water so that the earth is flooded? This tells us that God has complete control over the water supply on all the earth—including droughts, hurricanes, tornados, and floods! How's that for awesome power?

In Job 36:27-29 Elihu describes our atmosphere. Thousands of years later we marvel at His understanding of how God's power is involved in our weather. He said, "For he draws up the drops of water; they distill his mist in rain, 28 which the skies pour down and drop on mankind abundantly. 29 Can anyone understand the spreading of the clouds, the thunderings of his pavilion?" Man denies God's involvement in the weather and tries to explain it in scientific terms, but He still has complete control over all weather.

God's power is indescribable. Job teaches us an important lesson when discovering God's power. He says in part in 26:7–14, "He stretches out the north over the void and hangs the earth on nothing. 8 He binds up the waters in his thick clouds, and the cloud is not split open under them. 9 He covers the face of the full moon and spreads over it his cloud. 10 He has inscribed a circle on the face of the waters at the boundary between light and darkness. 11 The pillars of heaven tremble and are astounded at his rebuke. 12 By his power he stilled the sea; by his understanding he shattered Rahab. 13 By his wind the heavens were made fair; his hand pierced the fleeing serpent. 14 Behold, these are but the outskirts of his ways, and how small a whisper do we hear of him! But the thunder of his power who can understand?" We understand a small portion of His ways and cannot fathom the awesome power of a thunderbolt! Man today tries to describe these things in terms of scientific discoveries, and the sad thing is that they try to leave God out of the discussion, but He is right there in the middle of all weather phenomena and scientific discovery.

How does the Bible describe the extent of God's power? Psalm 104:32 gives us a graphic word-picture of the Lord's power: "who looks on the earth and it trembles, who touches the mountains and they smoke!" Or again in Psalm 97:4-5, which says, "His lightnings light up the world; the earth sees and trembles. [5] The mountains melt like wax before the LORD, before the Lord of all the earth." How is that for an awesome demonstration of unlimited power?

God's power boggles the mind. Many breathtaking descriptions of God's power and ability are found. For example, try this one—it boggles the mind: Isaiah 40:12 says, "Who has measured the waters in the hollow of his hand and marked off the heavens with a span, enclosed the dust of the earth in a measure and weighed the mountains in scales and the hills in a balance?" How can anyone measure the oceans of the world in the hollow of His hand? Such measurements of His awesome ability are hard to comprehend!

The scope of God's power is limitless. How far does His power extend? In answer to the question "How powerful is God—what can He do, and what does He have complete control over?" Daniel 2:21–23 answers: "He changes times and seasons; he removes kings and sets up kings; he gives wisdom to the wise and knowledge to those who have understanding; [22] he reveals deep and hidden things; he knows what is in the darkness, and the light dwells with him. [23] To you, O God of my fathers, I give thanks and praise, for you have given me wisdom and might, and have now made known to me what we asked of you, for you have made known to us the king's matter." So everything is under His complete control. Is He in control over every king, president, or prime minister on earth? In Daniel 6:26, King Darius says, "I make a decree, that in all my royal dominion people are to tremble and fear before the God of Daniel, for he is the living God, enduring forever; his kingdom shall never be destroyed, and his dominion shall be to the end." This describes His power coupled with His sovereignty in reigning over all the nations of the world.

God's power is incomprehensible. Psalm 18 describes in detail God's awesome strength and power. Here are a few excerpts from that great psalm: "The LORD is my rock and my fortress and my deliverer, my God, my rock, in whom I take refuge, my shield, and the horn of my salvation, my stronghold. . .then the earth reeled and rocked; the foundations also of the mountains trembled and quaked, because he was angry. . . the LORD also thundered in the heavens, and the Most High uttered his voice, hailstones and coals of fire. . .then the channels of the sea were seen, and the foundations of the world were laid bare at your rebuke, O LORD, at the blast of the breath of your nostrils." When these powerful acts of God are recorded, they are far beyond our comprehension. How He made this world, sustains it to this day, and uses it to control the whole earth is far beyond man's comprehension.

Can God do what man would think is impossible? The question "What is God able to do?" is answered by the angel speaking to Mary in Luke 1:37, telling her that she, a virgin, was going to become pregnant without the sperm implant of a man: "For with God nothing shall be impossible!" That simple sentence tells us that nothing is beyond the power of God.

God's power spoke this universe into existence. Genesis 1 simply says, "And God said..." and it was done. Hebrews 11:3 backs up this account when it says, "By faith we understand that the universe was created by the word of God, so that what is seen was not made out of things that are visible." Only faith understands that God can speak things into existence! Psalm 33:9 reiterates this when it says, "For he spoke, and it came to be; he commanded, and it stood firm." Psalm 29, speaking about God's power, might, glory, and holiness, says that God's voice holds the waters in place, brings thunder, is powerful and majestic, breaks cedars and makes them skip like a calf, divides flames of fire, shakes the desert, makes deer calve, and, in His temple, all speak about His glory. Psalm 46:6 completes this thought: "...he utters his voice, the earth melts."

What are some biblical examples of God's power in action?

Exodus 15 records Miriam's song after God totally destroyed the Egyptian army. Here are a few of the images from that chapter that chronicle the awesome power of God: The Lord cast Pharaoh, his chariots, his army, and his commanding officers to be drowned in the Red Sea. They sank like a stone. He dashed the enemies to pieces. With the blast of His breath, the waters gathered into a heap, and when the enemy decided to overtake the Israelites, again the wind blew and the sea waters covered the enemy. Neighboring nations will be amazed at the power of God, and their hearts will melt.

Numbers 11 records the Israelites complaining because of lack of food, specifically meat to eat. Here they were, all 600,000 men available for war, plus women and children (probably about three million people total). How was God going to provide enough meat to eat out there in the desert? He said to Moses in verse 23, "Is the Lord's hand waxed short? thou shalt see now whether my word shall come to pass unto thee or not." What he was saying is this: Is God not able to provide for them miraculously? Is He impotent and unable to take care of His children? Just watch and you will see whether His word will come to pass! Then it tells in the following verses how the Lord sent a wind that blew quail in from the surrounding sea that covered the camp for miles around with quail three feet deep!

What control does God have over man because of His power and sovereignty? In 1 Samuel 2:5b–10 Hannah's heart was bursting with praise to God after He gave her a son. Look at this list of the things God has power over in men's lives: "…The barren has borne seven, but she who has many children is forlorn. ^{6} The LORD kills and brings to life; he brings down to Sheol and raises up. ^{7} The LORD makes poor and makes rich; he brings low and he exalts. ^{8} He raises up the poor from the dust; he lifts the needy from the ash heap to make them sit with princes and inherit a seat of honor. For the pillars of the earth are the LORD's, and on them he has set the world. ^{9} He will guard the feet of his faithful ones, but the wicked shall be cut off in darkness, for not by might shall a man prevail. ^{10} The adversaries of the Lord shall be broken to pieces; against them he will thunder in heaven. The LORD will judge the ends of the earth; he will give strength to his king and exalt the horn of his anointed."

Wow, what a list! Adding to the list of the things God can do is found in 1 Chronicles 29:11–12: "Yours, O Lord, is the greatness and the power and the glory and the victory and the majesty, for all that is in the heavens and in the earth is yours. Yours is the kingdom, O Lord, and you are exalted as head above all. ^{12} Both riches and honor come from you, and you rule over all. In your hand are power and might, and in your hand it is to make great and to give strength to all."

God's power gives men confidence when facing overwhelming odds. As we read certain books of the Bible, we find a number of gems—a vast deposit of information—and this is true in 1 and 2 Chronicles. In 2

Chronicles 14:11, we find King Asa's prayer as he faced a huge army, one far bigger than his own army. Here's his prayer: "And Asa cried to the LORD his God, 'O LORD, there is none like you to help, between the mighty and the weak. Help us, O LORD our God, for we rely on you, and in your name we have come against this multitude. O LORD, you are our God; let not man prevail against you." How is that for confidence as King Asa faced a million-man Ethiopian army—which was totally defeated!

God's power is displayed when facing our enemies. First Samuel 7:7–13 is another example of the awesome power of God. One thing to note in Scripture, because it is repeated over and over, is that God uses forces that are at His disposal—and His alone—to wipe out our enemies. For example, do a study sometime on meteorology in the Scripture and look up words like *rain, hail, flood, drought, famine, lightning, thunder,* etc., and see how God used them—especially in defeating His enemies (and will yet use them greatly during the tribulation period). Here is one such illustration of this in a battle with the Philistines: "Now when the Philistines heard that the people of Israel had gathered at Mizpah, the lords of the Philistines went up against Israel. And when the people of Israel heard of it, they were afraid of the Philistines. [8] And the people of Israel said to Samuel, 'Do not cease to cry out to the LORD our God for us, that he may save us from the hand of the Philistines.' [9] So Samuel took a nursing lamb and offered it as a whole burnt offering to the LORD. And Samuel cried out to the LORD for Israel, and the LORD answered him. [10] As Samuel was offering up the burnt offering, the Philistines drew near to attack Israel. But the LORD thundered with a mighty sound that day against the Philistines and threw them into confusion, and they were defeated before Israel. [11] And the men of Israel went out from Mizpah and pursued the Philistines and struck them, as far as below Beth-car. [12] Then Samuel took a stone and set it up between Mizpah and Shen and called its name Ebenezer; for he said, 'Till now the LORD has helped us.' [13] So the Philistines were subdued and did not again enter the territory of Israel. And the hand of the LORD was against the Philistines all the days of Samuel."

Does God have complete power over the vast oceans and even the unrest in the world? Psalm 65:6–7 gives another example of what God can do. It says that God brought the mountains into existence by His strength—as He is clothed completely with power; He also stills the noise of the oceans and their waves and silences the tumult of an uprising.

God's power is magnificent and clearly seen when He comes to judge (see specifically the book of Revelation). The prophets of old tried to describe the greatness and the power of God, especially when He comes in judgment. Here's part of Habakkuk's prayer in 3:2–15 (notice how he searched for words to describe Almighty God when He comes to this earth)): "O LORD, I have heard the report of you, and your work, O LORD, do I fear. In the midst of the years revive it; in the midst of the years make it known; in wrath remember mercy. ³God came from Teman, and the Holy One from Mount Paran. *Selah* His splendor covered the heavens, and the earth was full of his praise. ⁴His brightness was like the light; rays flashed from his hand; and there he veiled his power. ⁵Before him went pestilence, and plague followed at his heels. ⁶He stood and measured the earth; he looked and shook the nations; then the eternal mountains were scattered; the everlasting hills sank low. His were the everlasting ways. ⁷I saw the tents of Cushan in affliction; the curtains of the land of Midian did tremble. ⁸Was your wrath against the rivers, O LORD? Was your anger against the rivers, or your indignation against the sea, when you rode on your horses, on your chariot of salvation? ⁹You stripped the sheath from your bow, calling for many arrows. *Selah* You split the earth with rivers. ¹⁰The mountains saw you and writhed; the raging waters swept on; the deep gave forth its voice; it lifted its hands on high. ¹¹The sun and moon stood still in their place at the light of your arrows as they sped, at the flash of your glittering spear. ¹²You marched through the earth in fury; you threshed the nations in anger. ¹³You went out for the salvation of your people, for the salvation of your anointed. You crushed the head of the house of the wicked, laying him bare from thigh to neck. *Selah* ¹⁴You pierced with his own arrows the heads of his warriors, who came like a whirlwind to scatter me, rejoicing as if to devour the poor in secret. ¹⁵You trampled the sea with your horses, the surging of mighty waters."

Next we need to recount the response of God's people, and the nations around them, when they see the great power of God displayed on behalf of His children. In other words, what does God do for each of His children as the world carefully watches us? Why are these many examples from Scripture important to us today?

God's power gives us boldness and confidence. Deuteronomy 7:21 gives us the reason we can be bold and not terrified by our enemies. God said to Israel through Moses, "You shall not be in dread of them, for the LORD your God is in your midst, a great and awesome God." Since He is such a powerful God and He resides with His people, why would we be intimidated? The world is intimidated and lets fear paralyze it; we must not let that happen!

God's power becomes a "refuge," a place of total protection. Deuteronomy 33:27 describes God as a refuge for us like this: "The eternal God is your dwelling place, and underneath are the everlasting arms. And he thrust out the enemy before you and said, 'Destroy.'"

God has chosen to show His power through His children. This is demonstrated in the account in Joshua where the waters of the Jordan River were dried up so the Israelites could cross over on dry ground. Joshua 4:23–24 says, "For the LORD your God dried up the waters of the Jordan for you until you passed over, as the LORD your God did to the Red Sea, which he dried up for us until we passed over, [24] so that all the peoples of the earth may know that the hand of the LORD is mighty, that you may fear the LORD your God forever." God still does many mighty things for His people so that the entire world may have visible demonstrations of what an invisible God can do!

Does God's power come through for us when we seek Him earnestly—like when we fast and pray? When Ezra and the people with him were to return to Judea, the question came up as to how they would be protected as they passed through dangerous lands with vast wealth to rebuild the temple. They could ask the king for protection, but they would be too embarrassed to do that. Ezra had told the king how his God was able to protect them, so this is what they did as recorded in 8:21–23: "Then I proclaimed a fast there, at the river Ahava, that we might humble ourselves before our God, to seek from him a safe journey for ourselves, our children, and all our goods. [22] For I was ashamed to ask the king for a band of soldiers and horsemen to protect us against the enemy on our way, since we had told the king, 'The hand of our God is for good on all who seek him, and the power of his wrath is against all who forsake him.' [23] So we fasted and implored our God for this, and he listened to our entreaty." What we must do, in following Ezra's example, is tell others that our God protects us because they are watching, and then we must ask God for the correct path to take and let the world around us see how God protects His children.

God's power is available to help us in everyday life. We long to see God's power at work in our daily life—helping us handle the frustrations, the grievances, and the burdens we all carry. Psalm 145:10–16 says: "All your works shall give thanks to you, O LORD, and all your saints shall bless you! [11] They shall speak of the glory of your kingdom and tell of your power, [12] to make known to the children of man your mighty deeds, and the glorious splendor of your kingdom. [13] Your kingdom is an everlasting kingdom, and your dominion endures throughout all generations. [The LORD is faithful in all his words and kind in all his works.] [14] The LORD upholds all who are falling and raises up all who are bowed down. [15] The eyes of all look to you, and you give them their food in due season. [16] You open your hand; you satisfy the desire of every living thing."

God's power protects us when the devil wants to destroy us. Jesus, in Matthew 10:28, tells us, "And do not fear those who kill the body but cannot kill the soul. Rather fear him who can destroy both soul and body in hell." That gives us great reassurance: Satan's restricted power can only kill the body; he has had the power of death (see Hebrews 2:14), but he can't send a person to hell forever in punishment! So God's power reassures those of us who fear Him and takes away the fear that the devil brings when he tries to scare us.

Does God's power make us stand in awe of Him and help us worship Him? In Ephesians 3:20–21 Paul tells us the immensity of God's power and what effect that power has on us: "Now to him who is able to do far more abundantly than all that we ask or think, according to the power at work within us, [21] to him be glory in the church and in Christ Jesus throughout all generations, forever and ever. Amen." Here Paul connects God's power with our overwhelming and never-ending response of praise and worship to Him who alone is worthy of our worship.

Seek

Next let's look at the power of God and learn how to tap into that power in our daily lives. Here are a few examples from the Scriptures:

Does God's power seen through us inspire others for many years to come? God gave Abraham a great big promise when He said to him, you will be the father of many nations. Problem was, Abraham and Sarah were childless. How would Abraham overcome that enormous hurdle? Romans 4:17–22 gives us the answer when speaking about Abraham: "as it is written, 'I have made you the father of many nations'—in the presence of the God in whom he believed, who gives life to the dead and calls into existence the things that do not exist. [18] In hope he believed against hope, that he should become the father of many nations, as he had been told, 'So shall your offspring be.' [19] He did not weaken in faith when he considered his own body, which was as good as dead (since he was about a hundred years old), or when he considered the barrenness of Sarah's womb. [20] No unbelief made him waver concerning the promise of God, but he grew strong in his faith as he gave glory to God, [21] fully convinced that God was able to do what he had promised. [22] That is why his faith was 'counted to him as righteousness.'" Wow! What a response of a fallen weak man to the unbelievable, overwhelming promise from Almighty God!

Believers long to see the power of God at work again and again in their lives. How do we tap into that power? What happens when we test God to see if He will come through for us? We must be careful of presumption, yet God challenges us "to test Him" or "prove Him" to see what He will do for His children. This challenge is given in Numbers 11:23 and Malachi 3:10, and in both passages we are told to test or prove God to see if He will come through on His word to us. His power is available to those who decide to honor Him (and in Malachi it was simply to pay their tithes to God), so test Him and see what He will do. Moses and the Israelites did in Numbers, and God fed them with quail abundantly in a desert where there were few if any quail. Since God's power is awesome, just test it and see for yourself.

When we face man's greatest foe, death, does God's power come through for us? For dying man, there is one great hope—everlasting life!

Why is that power so necessary for a person to grasp? Paul tells us in 2 Corinthians 13:4 that Jesus Christ "For he was crucified in weakness, but lives by the power of God. For we also are weak in him, but in dealing with you we will live with him by the power of God." God's resurrection power—demonstrated in Christ—is the inspiration for our hope. Because He lives, we also will live!

How does God's power clear up our theological questions? Note how Jesus explained the power of God when confronted with a theological question. When the religious leaders of Jesus' day came and asked Him about marriage in heaven and the resurrection, Jesus' answer was surprising. They had asked him whose wife would this woman would be when they got to heaven, who had (according to their made-up story) seven husbands here on earth. Before He answered them (in Mark 12:25), He told them that they were in error in this matter because they didn't know the Scriptures or the power of God. This answer would have been clear to them if they had two things straight: First, if they had known the Scriptures clearly, they would have understood that after the tribulation, after the second coming of Jesus Christ, and after the one-thousand-year reign of Christ when we are given our new final resurrection bodies, there will be no more marriage, cohabitating, and no more raising of children. Second, if they had known the power of God, they wouldn't have asked the question. The power of God explains to us that "nothing is impossible with God." We try hard to grapple with truth, but for our finite minds it seems that we can think of many things God can't do or won't do because it is part of His eternal plan. How many more of our questions would be answered if grasped fully the power of God?

Since we have taken a look at the subject of power, let's look at the other character qualities of God mentioned in Scripture along with power and see what insights we can glean. More than twenty-seven other character qualities of God are mentioned with His power, so it would seem that the power of God is central to all that He is, that is, from our human perspective. In fact, if He isn't powerful and all powerful, is He really God?

Here are a few character qualities of God that complement His power:

Is God's power displayed when He comes in wrath? Psalm 90:11 mentions God's anger and His wrath. If God weren't all powerful, someone somewhere could stand up at the time of judgment and say, "Oh no, You don't punish me!" But that will never happen. Psalm 78:40–49 gives us an account of His powerful deeds and then backs that up with the statement just made that He (God) throws the wicked down in the fierceness of His anger, wrath, and overpowering fury by sending evil angels among them—making a pathway for His anger.

Does God's power complement His sovereign control over the universe? Psalm 93:1 combines the power of God with His sovereign rule over everyone, and all demonstrated by the fact that the world is here to stay. It says, "The LORD reigns; he is robed in majesty; the LORD is robed; he has put on strength as his belt. Yes, the world is established; it shall never be moved."

How does the Bible tie together several attributes of God with His power? Psalm 145:4–9 says, "One generation shall commend your works to another, and shall declare your mighty acts. ⁵ On the glorious splendor of your majesty, and on your wondrous works, I will meditate. ⁶ They shall speak of the might of your awesome deeds, and I will declare your greatness. ⁷ They shall pour forth the fame of your abundant goodness and shall sing aloud of your righteousness. ⁸ The LORD is gracious and merciful, slow to anger and abounding in steadfast love. ⁹ The LORD is good to all, and his mercy is over all that he has made."

Nahum 1:3 gives our last glimpse here of several attributes of God combined in one verse: "The LORD is slow to anger and great in power, and the LORD will by no means clear the guilty. His way is in whirlwind and storm, and the clouds are the dust of his feet."

Why are God's infinite power and His infinite knowledge mentioned together? Jeremiah 10:12 and 51:15 are identical. They say, "It is he who made the earth by his power, who established the world by his wisdom, and by his understanding stretched out the heavens." In fact, His knowledge is so vast—as we will see later—it is infinite, and man will never be able to comprehend it! If any other being in the universe had more knowledge than God or knowledge in one area that God didn't have, that being would be more powerful that God. So both His knowledge and His power have to be infinite and immeasurable.

Man may ask, "Are there some things God cannot do?" The answer is this: As far as His ability is concerned, He can do anything and all things; yet there are certain things He *will not* do because they violate His character and His program for this world and sinful man. Ability speaking, God could wipe out all evil instantaneously, or He could have never allowed sin to exist in the first place. If He did that, then we wouldn't be able to comprehend His righteousness, His holiness, or the fierceness of His anger against sin. So His plan to explain Himself to man is to give us a number of attributes, or character qualities, and through them explain to finite man more and more about Himself! This is the wonder of what we will be discovering eternally.

If we know His great power, what are we to do with the knowledge of it? Right now we see His power coming to our rescue and delivering us when the devil and the world would try to wipe us out. All that we see about His power leads us into worshipping Him. Here's a good question: Will we see a never-ending unfolding of the power of God as we move into eternity? Many people are nervous about what is going to happen in eternity. The word *hallelujah* is found nowhere else in the Bible until we get to Revelation 19:1–6, but when we go from this earth into eternity and prepare to spend eternity serving and worshipping God, it is used in the following passage four times. Notice how central God's power is mentioned: "After this I heard what seemed to be the loud voice of a great multitude in heaven, crying out, 'Hallelujah! Salvation and glory and power belong to our God, [2] for his judgments are true and just; for he has judged the great prostitute who corrupted the earth with her immorality, and has avenged on her the blood of his servants." [3] Once more they cried out, 'Hallelujah! The smoke from her goes up forever and ever.' [4] And the twenty-four elders and the four living creatures fell down and worshiped God who was seated on the throne, saying, 'Amen. Hallelujah!' [5] And from the throne came a voice saying, 'Praise our God, all you his servants, you who fear him, small and great.[6] Then I heard what seemed to be the voice of a great multitude, like the roar of many waters and like the sound of mighty peals of thunder, crying out, 'Hallelujah! For the Lord our God the Almighty reigns.'" This is what we have to look forward to in eternity—remembering how God in His great power delivered us from sin and death, cleaned us up completely, and now we get the privilege of exalting Him forever!

How does one character quality of God ignite the praise of God's children? Psalm 21:13 says, "Be exalted, O LORD, in your strength! We will sing and praise your power." This is what ignites our praise and becomes the theme of our song—His mighty power! Note also how many of the stories of the great victories the Israelites enjoyed are followed by a song or an outburst of praise (such as the crossing of the Red Sea and the drowning of the Egyptian army). We are instructed to praise God for His mighty power, and that isn't hard when we see His mighty power at work. Here's the point: When we look at each character quality, something in that quality begs our praise and our worship of Him. All of them point to a God who is so awesome and powerful and holy and loving, etc., and each of them ignites our praise more and more as we see them demonstrated in our lives daily. He is great and greatly to be praised!

Worship

Pause to Praise and Worship: Almighty God, we stand in awe of your power; we see it as You demonstrated it for Your people throughout the Bible, and we see it active in our lives on a daily basis. Where would we be without Your power coming to our aid every day and every hour of every day? We bow and worship You because we see ourselves as so finite—especially in power—and we see You as omnipotent. Demonstrate that power again and again in our lives to remind us of who You are and how much love You have for us as Your children. We know that if we weren't Your children, Your power would be used against us and not for us. So we bow and worship You as the One who defined power, and we look forward to worshipping You forever for Your great, awesome, infinite, and overwhelming power.

Chapter 5

Truth: Man's Rock of Gibraltar

John 14:6: "Jesus said to him, "I am the way, and the truth, and the life. No one comes to the Father except through me."

- Man is searching for truth, but where does he find it?
- Is the best this world has to offer a fast-paced, changing world?
- Why does the world have to change so much?
- Is there anything anywhere that man can put his trust in that is "absolute"?
- Pilate said it best when he said rhetorically: "What is truth?"
- On what "solid rock" can man build his life?

As I carefully studied the many character qualities of God, I often wondered which one would end up meaning the most. Certainly to a sinful, wicked, evil, vile, proud, and desperately sick sinner, the holiness of God should shine as the brightest to man. Or consider that man in his sinful and lost condition desperately needs the love, mercy, and forgiveness of God. What about the character qualities of man that he is totally devoid of, like omniscience or omnipresence? Certainly these should shine as bright stars to a finite being like man! But what character quality of God ended up being the one most needed by this author to put the Scriptures in perspective as the eternal Word of God?

When considering all the qualities of God together, the one that ended up being the shining light to my heart was this: God is the God of truth—He is Truth! Man lives in a fast-paced and ever-changing world.

Technology and knowledge are changing so fast these days that a person can get the most advanced degree available and the best training available in the world, yet what that person learned is obsolete in a short period of time. You can buy the best and most expensive high-tech device, but it is often out of date in a few days, and before it wears out, it is badly outdated. The information gleaned from scientific research each day can fill several encyclopedias!

Not only are science and technology changing fast, but also our world changes fast in many other ways—from the political, to current events, to the way of doing business, to the way the world responds to one another. These things change fast and on a daily basis. Investments that look quite secure can evaporate in a short period of time. Relationships change, many times quickly. With this many changes in our world, is anything unchangeable that man can cling to?

Thankfully, the Christian can cling to one unchangeable thing—the truth of God. Like the proverbial "rock of Gibraltar," man can look to God for things that do not change. God's truth is absolute. It cannot change because He does not change; it cannot be changed because, if it did, it wouldn't be truth. For most of mankind, things change so fast, and everything is so uncertain, and all because man has rejected the absolute truth of God revealed in His Holy Word.

In today's world man has repeated the lie that there are no absolutes, and everything is relative—all of which leads to absurdity. We know where every lie comes from, and they all come from the father of lies—the devil (see John 8:44). The closer a person gets to God and accepting the truth of God as an absolute that he can totally trust, the closer he gets to seeing this world only as a fleeting mirage—a life that is quickly passing away with its lusts and desire. Man must become aware of the fact that "he that does the will of God will live forever."

Know

What do the Scriptures mean when they say that God is a "God of truth"? God's truth is unchangeable. It means that I can trust Him to do what He said He would do. God swore "in truth" to David in Psalm 132:11 that

He would always have a descendant of David on the throne, and He never turned back from that promise. In Numbers 23:19 we are told that God is not like a man who changes constantly; that is, He cannot change, lie, or repent. Only changeable man can do those things. But God does not and cannot change! We find God referred to several times in the Scripture as the "unchangeable God" (such as 1 Samuel 15:29), and if God did change in regard to who He is and what His character is, then He would cease to be God! Again and again the Scripture emphasizes to us, "I am the Lord; I do not change!" This includes all of His eternal attributes—and especially to the truth of God.

God's truth means that He will always keep His word to us. We are told in those same two verses that only God has the ability to bring about what He says He will do. When He makes a promise, He can also fulfill that promise, while man has a hard time keeping his word from one day to another.

God's truth assures us that it will never change. God deals with man in truth, and the way He deals with us never changes. God deals with man in righteousness, an upright way, and without injustice, and that will never change! Deuteronomy 32:4 gives one of the names of God as "the God of Truth," and Revelation 15:3b says, "Great and amazing are your deeds, O Lord God the Almighty! Just and true are your ways, O King of the nations." This God of truth *is* the absolute standard for everyone everywhere, and He alone reveals that truth to man. The exciting thing about this is the way Jesus Christ, His Son, introduced Himself to us in John 14:6 as "I am . . . the truth!"

Can we trust God's truth to guide us each day? Imagine being guided in life by Someone who cannot change from day to day. Psalm 25:10 refers to the ways or the paths of the Lord as "mercy and truth." When I, as His child, walk in His ways, I will always run into His mercy and His truth; they will be my constant companions throughout life. Psalm 43:3 tells us God's truth and light leads me to the feet of the King of kings and Lord of lords in worship!

Psalm 138:2 tells us that we are led in worship and praise by God's loving-kindness and His truth. Why are these two qualities mentioned together often? It is because man's greatest need, as a sinful and dying creature, is to be shown love and mercy (the Old Testament puts these two together as "loving-kindness") for a God who will never change or take them away from us. If God ever failed to show His love and mercy toward us, where would we be? If He ever changed, where would we be? So these two together assure us that His love will always be there for us.

How is God's mercy affected by the fact that He is truth? When God deals with man in line with His unchangeable truth, man could easily be swallowed up and wiped out if God didn't also deal with man in mercy. In Psalm 57:3; 86:15; 89:14; 25:10; 100:4; 117:2; and 108:4, mercy and truth are mentioned together as attributes of God. "God is truth" means that He is good, right, holy, and righteous, and these things never change. When we find that "God is mercy," we discover that He has found a way wipe out man's sin so that man can enjoy the presence of God forever, and that will never change! He has sent forth His truth, and it has reached down to the lowest sinner, and because of His mercy, that lost sinner can become a saint!

How is God's truth contrasted with the lies of the devil? Psalm 33:4 tells us that all of God's works are 100 percent accurate. By contrast, Satan relies on deceit, deception, lies, and getting man to change by offering him something different or even better. That's what he did in the Garden of Eden when he tried to offer Adam and Eve something better than what God had already offered and given them. God's truth assures us that He cannot change. His laws are 100 percent accurate and don't need revising. He does nothing that is not in lockstep with his truth!

How does God's truth change our perspective on everything? Psalm 33:4 tells us, "All His work is done in truth," (JKV) or according to His eternal character. When He created this world, it wasn't haphazard or chaotic. It may look that way to man in the middle of the construction campaign that this world is now in, but when it is finished, we will marvel forever at the masterpiece God has built. We can spread a jigsaw puzzle out on table and begin to work on it, and it looks chaotic and impossible to piece together; but as we look at the picture on the outside of the box and piece it together according to the pattern or picture, it fits together piece by piece. As we look at this unfinished world in which we live, we can become disheartened or discouraged because we can't yet see the picture on the outside of the box, that is unless we spend much time poring over His eternal Word, see the "truth" in it, and bit by bit get a fuller picture of the awesome God we serve. Someday in eternity, when we see the entire puzzle of God's purposes unfolded, we will marvel and rejoice forever for His great "mercy and truth" as He has given it to us in the Bible!

Can man conceal his excitement when he gets hold of the truth of God coupled with His loving-kindness? In Psalm 40:10 is the testimony of King David, who was so excited about the "loving-kindness and truth" of God he couldn't conceal it from crowds of people. Is there anyone in Scripture who taught us more about how to worship God than King David in the Psalms? Probably not! When we see from Scripture the overwhelming love of God and the absolute truth of God, no person can hold back. This is a great incentive to worship God forever!

How does God's truth become a shield to us? Psalm 91:4 says, "He will cover you with his pinions, and under his wings you will find refuge; his faithfulness is a shield and buckler." (God's truth and His faithfulness are often seen together.) When I see God as the God of truth that is absolute and unchangeable, that becomes a shield to me because I can now and forever rest in the fact that, even though man around me changes, my environment changes, my circumstances change, my finances always change, my life changes, and someday I will be totally changed from a sinful, dying creature into a beloved son of God that will live fully righteous in His presence forever; yet still He remains the same yesterday, today, and forever. His eternal truth shields me from my changing world! So the ultimate security protection system for man is the truth of God. Everything may change; in fact, "but whoever does the will of God abides forever." So the person who does the will of God is ultimately protected and will never cease to exist (see 1 John 2:15-18).

God's truth never changes eternally. We are assured of this in both Psalm 100:5 and Psalm 117:2. It will always be there for me because it is eternal as He is, and I can rely on Him and His truth forever.

Can I can commit everything into God's hands because His truth never changes? Since He purchased me and redeemed me with His blood, Psalm 31:5 tells me I can commit my spirit into His hands. What in life can men commit themselves to? A cause? A man? A good work? A destiny?

This verse points out to us that the only One, or the only thing, a godly man or woman can commit themselves to outside this life is the "God of truth"! Everything else is temporal and will lead to a horrible destiny.

Why do I keep repeating the fact that God's truth is unchangeable? His truth is absolute (in a world longing for absolutes); it cannot change because if it did change, it wouldn't be the "truth of God" anymore. For man to see that His truth cannot change eternally is a great comfort to the believer and gives him something to "hang his hat on" that will never change!

Can God's truth be our daily guide? Psalm 86:11 says, "Teach me your way, O Lord, that I may walk in your truth; unite my heart to fear your name." My life must be centered on the truth of God's Word and then guide every step I take as I walk with Him day by day. Can anything else be the guide of a true believer? Only God's unchanging truth can guide a lost sinner into a right relationship with a holy God and then lead that believer into eternity to live with God forever.

The truth of God constantly purifies our lives. John 17:17 says, "Sanctify them in the truth; your word is truth." When we are sanctified, we are purified and renewed. The only way my life is purified continually is when I absorb the Word as I daily walk with God. His Word purifies my heart and mind because it is truth. When His Word is purifying my heart, then changes that are made are the eternal changes I need.

How is the truth of God revealed through the person of Jesus? John 8:12–48 records a lengthy discourse between Jesus and the Pharisees. Jesus began the discussion by asserting, "I am the light of the world," and everything else is darkness. The Pharisees shot back that His authenticity was based on Himself. In the verses that follow, Jesus contrasted "the truth" with "the lie." Jesus' life contrasted for us the difference between the truth and the lie: all lies come from the father of lies, the devil. He asserted that He is the truth of God and what He said was truth. Bottom line: everything Jesus was and taught reflected the truth of God. The message was clear, and when they rejected Him, they were rejecting the truth of God. So Jesus' life and words personified the truth of God.

Think of Jesus Christ, the truth of God, this way: every religion in the world has a leader or a founder, and their followers claim that he was a "good person." But Jesus' claim that "I am the way, the truth, and the life" puts Him as the only One who could truly make that claim. Man needed the life of a Man who was holy and sinless and who would set the pristine example of a pure life. This One would need to come from God and demonstrate to everyone what we could be like with the grace of God fully operative in our lives, and this is clearly seen in Jesus' life. John 1:14 says, "And the Word became flesh and dwelt among us, and we have seen his glory, glory as of the only Son from the Father, full of grace and truth."

How does the fact that God is truth hold us in life's battle with the foe? In Ephesians 6:14, one of the outstanding applications of the truth of God is this: when we accept the truth of God as ours, this verse tells us that this is how we stand firm in the Christian life; that is, when we have the belt of the truth of God's Word firmly holding in place the rest of the armor. This is significant because Paul was saying that we are in a fierce battle with satanic forces, and if we are going to make it through victoriously, then the truth around our waists *will hold everything together!* This is a good analogy because it shows the vital part the truth of God plays in whether we walk victoriously or are in constant defeat. So when we are in a skirmish with the devil and we find ourselves losing ground, then we must check to see where we abandoned the truth of God and get it back in place—and only then will we again be able to "stand firm" in the battle every Christian is facing.

Will God's truth finally triumph over the evil in this world? In the climax book of the Bible, the book of Revelation, we find that we can fully trust God, who is holy and true, to judge and avenge us for all the evil done to us by this lost and sinful world (15:3). Will justice ever be done here on earth? Will I ever be vindicated here and now? No! Only when the Judge comes and sets the books straight and judges all evil and totally wipes it out will I be properly avenged for all the evil done against me! Then we will see God's truth triumph once and for all. Therefore, since God is true and has revealed His truth, I can fully trust Him! His truth will reign!

Seek

The final point to make here is this: how does God's character, the fact that He is truth, help me in everyday life?

1. God's truth helps me turn away from sin as God has commanded me to do. In Daniel 9:13, Daniel is confessing the sins of his people when he says this: "As it is written in the Law of Moses, all this calamity has come upon us; yet we have not entreated the favor of the LORD our God, turning from our iniquities and gaining insight by your truth." Daniel made clear that because we have abandoned God's truth, disasters come on us, and when we confess and turn from our sins, then we begin to understand that our God is "the God of Truth."

2. God's truth shines through our failures and sin. In Romans 3:7–8, Paul condemns those who say that since glory comes to God through our sins and failures, then we should just sin all the more. So, is God glorified more when He gets glory through my sins and failures, or does God get more glory when I turn from sin and allow the truth of God to prevail in my personal life? The Bible never tells us that we are better off to sin more and more; we are better off when God's truth cleanses our lives. God is glorified when His truth wins out and my sin and my failure are fully dealt with—and that happened at the cross. That's why we glory in the cross, where cleansing through Jesus' blood comes to us.

3. One point to reemphasize here is that God's truth guides us throughout life. We look daily into the Word and find more guidance—what to do, what not to do, how to live, wisdom in making decisions, and to sort out all of the intricacies of life and use God's wisdom and truth to be our final authority and guide.

4. The closing emphasis to the truth of God is to reemphasize that it is the only eternal thing we can solidly build our lives on, and that is why God gave us His truth. His truth sets us free! His truth holds our lives and our future together. His truth is found only

in His Word. His truth is the anchor of our souls. Hang on tight until we see His truth prevail; it's going to be quite a ride!

We have talked before about the bumpy ride we take through life because much in this world is based on lies—and especially lies that come from the evil one. Yet as we struggle to understand the truth of God, we find footing in patterning our lives after the truth and the God of truth revealed in the Bible. This gives us one more reason to worship our great God, the fact that He is truth, He is absolute truth, His truth is unchanging, and His truth is eternal gives us something solid to build our lives on. It also energizes us more and more to praise Him and worship Him for giving us something absolute to live by and hang on to in an ever-changing world.

Worship

Pause to Praise and Worship: O God, you have told us that the most important thing we can do as a Christian is to worship You, and You give us so many reasons to practice worship and praise. You gave us Your eternal Word, and in it You unveiled to us Your eternal and unchanging truth. You didn't leave us to wonder for sure what truth is; You revealed it and then gave us many examples of godly men and women in the Bible who lived by the truth revealed to them. Thank You for their examples because they are all in heaven with You now because they responded to the truth revealed to them. We too grasp hold of the truth revealed to us, and for it we worship and praise You—as we will do forever!

Chapter 6

Judge/Judgment: Devastating and Coming Soon

Romans 14:12: "So then each of us will give an account of himself to God."

- What characteristics of God are revealed when He comes to judge?
- If God does judge man, what criteria does He use?
- Will God judge all nations of the world?
- How does God show that He is just and the final judge of all men?
- Have some nations been thoroughly judged already?
- What happens if all nations got together and stood up in unison against the judge?
- What is the final end of God's judgment on all who have rebelled against Him?
- Does God judge Christians too? And what happens to them after they are judged?

These questions make each of us stop in our tracks and contemplate seriously the fact that all men will be judged; they quickly make us think soberly. These questions are far beyond the scope of this book to answer completely, so we will look at the character qualities of God revealed during judgment and see how these traits and characteristics tell us a lot about our Judge. God has chosen to reveal much about Himself through times of judgment, so our design is to look at the judgments of God recorded in Scripture (and the ones that are yet coming for us) and see how through them God revealed Himself. In our world today many court cases are purposely brought up before certain judges and/or filed in certain courts because they believe they will have a more favorable ruling based on the judge they will face. Since we will all have to face "the final Judge," it will help us know beforehand the setting for that trial and much more about the One we will stand before on that day.

Know

From the beginning of time, man has had the sense that he will someday have to face a judge for all he has done here on earth. Many people on their deathbed reportedly want to make things right with others around them, probably because they know they are about to meet their Maker. When God gave that one command to Adam and Eve, He immediately put in that command their sentence if they disobeyed, saying, "And the LORD God commanded the man, saying, 'You may surely eat of every tree of the garden, ¹⁷ but of the tree of the knowledge of good and evil you shall not eat, for in the day that you eat of it you shall surely die.'" (Genesis 2:16–17). In that statement God passed on the death sentence for every man, and in doing so also revealed His righteous character, and so when man violated that command, they waited to fall over dead immediately. When that didn't happen, they soon figured out that now there was a spiritual separation from God, a spiritual death that occurred, and when Cain killed Abel, they then understood what physical death was.

God chose to reveal Himself in many ways, and times of judgment are just one of those ways. With this in mind, let's look at the various ways God has revealed Himself during times of judgment. The major judgments of God recorded in the Bible along with the ones we know are coming will be enough to help us see much about our great God. These facts are sobering but necessary for every person to face. (The words in *italics* point out the various character qualities of God that are tied to judgment.)

The first judgment of God recorded in Scripture is the great flood of Noah's day (and here we will list only some of the judgments recorded for us). The first fifteen hundred years or so of history went by, and nothing on earth seemed to be going right, so God decided it was time to step in and show man once and for all that he *must be prepared to meet his Judge*. This immediately points out to us the *long-suffering patience* of our God in waiting so long for man to turn from his evil ways. To further emphasize this, God told Noah to build an ark and to preach about God's *righteousness* so as to point out to man where he went wrong. Noah preached this message of righteousness for one hundred years, which again emphasizes how patient and long-suffering God is when dealing with man. Since the time of the garden of Eden, Adam and Eve knew they had violated God's command, and so did every person born after that, and now the judgment of the great flood emphasized that man must be prepared to meet his Maker—and his Judge.

During the flood every person alive on earth (except the eight who were safe in the ark) was wiped out, and the way God chose to do it was left for Noah pass down to succeeding generations to record. He knew the awesome *power* of God that was unleashed as God broke up the earth's crust, and with the huge volumes of water in the atmosphere and the water below the earth's surface, He flooded the entire world. When bringing judgment, God has demonstrated His complete control over all of what man mistakenly calls "the laws of nature." They include upheavals of the earth's crust as "the fountains of the great deep were opened up" and "the windows of heaven were opened." This demonstrates His complete command of all meteorological forces such as rain, wind, flood, and waters above, on, and under the earth's surface. These are His laws and evidences of His mighty power. And when the flood was over, God raised up the earth's crust and created the mountains and the surface of the earth as we know it today. What awesome *power* on display! In the story of the great flood, we also see the *kindness* and *protection* of God for His children when Noah and His family were safe in the ark.

The second judgment recorded is when God rained "fire and brimstone" down on several cities that had gone into perverted and devious sexual misconduct. Here is how God chose to reveal His character during this judgment: this time, instead of using flood waters, God chose to demonstrate His power by what we today would describe like an atomic bomb. Again it is because people had offended His *holiness*, and

He demonstrated what is right and wrong to man by pointing out His righteousness.

In each of the judgments recorded in Scripture, God uses a different plan each time, but He does show His *mercy* and *compassion* in saving those who had placed their faith in Him. In this instance we are informed that Lot was a righteous man, and God preserved his life and the life of his two daughters. (The complete story is recorded in references to Sodom and Gomorrah in Genesis 10:19; 13:10, 13; 14; and 18:16–19:26.)

One of the interesting things to note in this account is how God responded in compassion to the "outcry" He heard coming from the only two righteous men in the area—Lot and Abraham. Because of this outcry, God Himself came down to see how bad things were in those cities, and two of His angels were sent to rescue Lot from certain destruction.

The third major judgment came when God sent His own special nation into captivity for their sins. God did show *compassion* and *mercy* for the remnant whose lives were spared, but He also showed His *holy* and *righteous* character by bringing judgment on them even though they were His own special people.

When we see how God showed compassion and mercy on the remnant, we can ask and answer several questions: first, is God *just* and fair in giving man a warning when judgment is about to fall? Yes, many prophets came and told long before the judgment fell that it was coming, and then when the time of judgment came, other prophets came to reemphasize the warning. Second, how does God show *compassion and mercy* and His *wrath* at the same time? For a time God spared the southern kingdom of Judah and gave them more time to repent. Then a way to escape the coming slaughter was to defect to the Babylonians and/or be taken captive like Ezekiel, Daniel, Daniel's three friends, and a great number of those who took God seriously.

One other thought here: did the world around God's people laugh and scorn when He came to judge them? Yes, and according to Obadiah 10, the nation of Edom was completely wiped out because they helped the surrounding nations and didn't give any Israelites refuge when the captivity came.

Here are a few verses from Nahum 1:2–6 that graphically describe God's character during this time of judgment: "The LORD is a jealous and avenging God; the LORD is avenging and wrathful; the LORD takes vengeance on his adversaries and keeps wrath for his enemies. ³ The LORD is slow to anger and great in power, and the LORD will by no means clear the guilty. His way is in whirlwind and storm, and the clouds are the dust of his feet. ⁴ He rebukes the sea and makes it dry; he dries up all the rivers; Bashan and Carmel wither; the bloom of Lebanon withers. ⁵ The mountains quake before him; the hills melt; the earth heaves before him, the world and all who dwell in it. ⁶ Who can stand before his indignation? Who can endure the heat of his anger? His wrath is poured out like fire, and the rocks are broken into pieces by him."

The fourth judgment was the pouring out of the *wrath* of God on His own Son. God chose to pour out His wrath on His own Son when Jesus took our sins on Himself on the cross. Does that seem just and fair to us? This is no doubt one of the hardest things in the Bible to understand, but if God poured out His wrath on sinners who deserved eternal punishment, no one could ever be saved. So how could His righteous wrath against sin be satisfied? The only way was to place our sins on Jesus so that we could avoid God's wrath forever. Paul summed this up in 2 Corinthians 5:21 when he said, "For our sake he made him to be sin who knew no sin, so that in him we might become the righteousness of God."

The Great Tribulation is the fifth judgment. What is significant about this revelation of God's character is that He has chosen to unveil His Son, Jesus Christ, as the final judge. Yes, He will deal with His chosen people and bring them to repentance, and He will also deal harshly with those nations who have been part of scattering the Jews all over the world and have divided "My land," the nation of Israel. During this time of intense world upheaval, God will destroy the wicked and purify the world and prepare it for a time of peace under the Prince of peace.

One thing to note in the tribulation is how God uses His immense power. Mentioned in Revelation are a number of earthquakes, stars falling from heaven, floods, and great hail—and these are just a few examples of God's awesome power when His wrath is poured out on mankind. This time in history can only be described as catastrophic and massive upheaval and apocalyptic.

The Judgment Seat of Christ (or the Bema) is the sixth judgment mentioned in Scripture. Again we ask and answer the question: is God *just* and fair when He insists that His people have to face a time of judgment for what they have done? Second Corinthians 5:10 tells us, "For we must all appear before the judgment seat of Christ, so that each one may receive what is due for what he has done in the body, whether good or evil." It is good to note at the outset of this discussion that the eternal destiny of everyone at this time of judgment has already been decided. Everyone here is bound for an eternity in heaven with God, so this judgment is primarily to receive rewards for those who have "overcome" and have been "good and faithful servants."

God is both *holy and just*, and each person who has entered the presence of God forever must be totally cleansed, and they must be holy and righteous forever. If pride is the number one sin of demonic forces and man's number one sin, then at some point—possibly here at the judgment seat of Christ—some will "be ashamed before Him at His coming," but all of us will come at some point to the place where sanctification will be complete, and each person will be totally humbled and broken before God. Only then will we be ready to reflect His love and mercy forever, which is the reason we were created.

The seventh major judgment is the Battle of Armageddon. The question to ask here is this: will God reveal His great wrath, power, and judgment when all people on earth and all the demonic forces launch one last battle against God? This is what the Battle of Armageddon is all about as described in Revelation 19. Satan will be released out of the "bottomless pit" for a brief time, and we read, "...the kings of the earth with their armies, gathered together to make war against him who was sitting on the horse and against his army." At that time Jesus Christ, the Judge of all the earth, will come at that time on a white horse with all believers on earth following Him. No one on our side has to fight in this battle because a sword comes out of the mouth of Jesus Christ and totally destroys all unbelievers and all demonic forces.

The Great White Throne Judgment is the eighth and final judgment mentioned in Scripture. This judgment points out God's justice and fairness as He judges one last and final time. Many people today believe they will get to heaven on the basis of their own merit or good works, and all false religions of the world are built on a system of "good works," and this is the judgment for them. Each person will be individually examined and judged according to each thing they did when here on earth. Then their names are cross-referenced in the "book of life" to see if their names are "blotted out of the book of life." Then, as each person stands before the final judge of all time, they are each sentenced, and all are cast into the lake of fire and brimstone forever. This is a sobering thought, but it points out how God has, in His righteous character, given each person one final last chance, and for those who have decided to stand before God on their own merit, they will all lose.

Seek

One question we can ask is this: what indications are there that the judgment of God is imminent? Here are a few clues:

- An outcry comes from that area. In Abraham's time the outcry must have come from the only two righteous men mentioned that lived in that area: Abraham and Lot.
- God's people (in the case mentioned above, it was His prophet, Abraham) plead with God for mercy on the righteous that lived in that area where the judgment was to fall.
- In the case of the time just before Noah's flood, the wickedness of mankind was widespread and great.
- When evil is at its height, the wrath of God is poured out in judgment.
- From the record in Revelation, there are various scenes in heaven where activity was taking place: messages came from the throne; angels were scurrying about; and preparations were made for the next series of judgments to be poured out.

As we conclude this section, let's see again how God's righteous character is revealed. The bottom line is this: God is the one and only final judge.

He alone has the ability to see the "thoughts and intentions" of the heart of each person as described in Hebrews 4:12–13. Only an all-knowing God has that ability to know all there is to know about each person and justly and righteously sentence them. His judicial decision is final—there will be no appeals, and again and again in Scripture we are told that "there is no partiality with God."

As we look at God's character and judgment, we are struck with His holiness and purity—that is, He is totally free from sin. In many of the rest of the character qualities of God, man can claim to have a little of them: for instance, God has all power, and man has a little power; God has unfailing and unconditional *love*, but man has just a little love, the "if you love me then I will love you" kind of love; God is present everywhere, but man can be present in only one place at a time. But when it comes to God's holiness, man is totally devoid of it. Paul tells us, "as it is written: 'None is righteous, no, not one; [11] no one understands; no one seeks for God." (Romans 3:10–11). The challenge that each Christian faces is to watch God make each of us holy as He is holy, and that means Him putting His righteousness into each believer so we can be holy. In judgment God reveals His ultimate holy character for the whole universe to see.

Another point to make is this: when the judgments of God are complete, then all wickedness and sin and evil will be abolished forever— we will never have to contend with it again. This is great news for us because the battle we now face is with the forces of evil, but one day that battle will be over! Hallelujah!

In all of this, the justice, the judgment, the impartiality, and the awesome power of God are revealed in each judgment. The rainbow of His character qualities is constantly unfolded as He shows His longsuffering attitude, His love, His judgment on evil, and yet His grace in those times of judgments when He thoroughly purifies His children and prepares them to minister to Him throughout all eternity. What a privilege to be one of those whom He has chosen to set His love on! To be part of those throughout all of eternity that will showcase His mercy, His love, and His forgiveness! I can't think of any higher privilege than to reflect His marvelous character forever!

Worship

Pause to Praise and Worship: O God, every man shudders when he thinks about having to stand before One who sees right through him and knows all about him, including his thoughts and motives. Yet we must get serious about it because the day will come, and each of us must be ready. Thank You for loving us and sending Your Son to die for our sins and thus providing a way to avoid forever the penalty of our sins. We know that judgment day is awful, yet we can come before You all cleaned up, having thoroughly turned away from our sin and cleansed by the blood of Christ, and then experience boldness as we await the day when we will have our appearance before You. Help us be quick and ruthless in dealing with sin in our lives and repent and confess our sin quickly so we can be ready to stand before You.

As this world faces judgment during the tribulation, we don't relish the fact that we may be alive and watch some of the awful plagues come—either from here on earth or in heaven with You, but they all point to the fact that You are *righteous* and *holy* and that Your wrath must come as a result of man's sin. Teach us to stand back and stand firm in a pure and holy life that lets You be the sovereign God and judge when and where You see fit. We don't want to see our world crumble and fall, yet it is necessary in Your will and plan for this world. When judgment does come, may our hearts be broken, just like Jeremiah as he wept to see his nation destroyed.

Chapter 7

Access: Open and Available

Ephesians 2:18: "For through him (Jesus) we both have access in one Spirit to the Father."

- How can we come close to a God we can't see?
- How far away is He?
- Why doesn't He just move His throne down here so we can be near Him?
- If we were to draw close to God, who would have to take the initiative to make it happen?
- If I try hard enough and seek long enough, can I approach Him?
- Do only certain people or priests or ministers have access to God?
- If God and I were close, what would change about my life?
- What would it take to open the door of "total access" to God?

Man fumbles through life with these questions often haunting him. Most people on earth (and the last I heard over 95 percent in America) believe that God does indeed exist, but the problem comes when one tries to find Him. Where could a person go, or where do I start on my journey to find God? Many people feel like this journey will take them all of their lives, but they haven't examined God's book, the Bible, for the answer to these questions.

A person can search all his life and come up short in finding God because he or she looked in the wrong way or in the wrong places. Romans 3:10-11 stops the search cold in its tracks because it tells us, "as it is written:

'None is righteous, no, not one; no one understands; no one seeks for God.'" Why is that so? The apostle Paul went on to explain why in the rest of the chapter when he tells us that all of us have sinned and fall far short of reaching the glory of God's presence. The point Paul makes is this: if you are aware of your sin and your sinful inner nature, you are on the right road, but you are spiritually dead and have no basis on which to approach God.

Let's now turn in this chapter and see the character qualities of God alongside some words used to describe Him and His relationship to us. Here is one: *access*. So, then, where does access to God begin? First, man must be aware of, and admit to God, his own sinful condition. Second, each person will be drawn to God by Jesus Christ Himself. This is God's love reaching out to a lost world—to all in the world as He is not willing that *any* should perish but that *all* should come to a point of turning about-face from one's sin and to God in faith. Third, God's gift of eternal life is extended by grace and by grace alone to obtain the greatest gift a dying person could ever hope for—the gift of eternal life. One must "be saved by grace through faith" (Ephesians 2:8–9) as he or she reaches up in faith to accept that gift. John 1:12 describes it this way: "But to all who did receive him, who believed in his name, he gave the right to become children of God." Then what a transformation takes place, and then access is opened up to God the Father! Without this access granted by salvation, no one has access to God.

Know

So who in the Bible had access to God, and how did they get it? Let's look at several passages that show how access to God came.

Accessibility to God came through His chosen people (Deuteronomy 4:7). Through these words from Moses, we find out that the only nation so great that God is near them is God's chosen people, Israel. God is available to all of them who call on Him. Moses' point is this: access to God began much earlier than this, as God personally visited many people, but ultimate access to God became available to all people everywhere through God's choice of Israel as a nation. They had a special closeness to God, which was the envy of the world!

Accessibility to God comes only when God seeks man. In Psalm 43:3–4 the psalmist beckons to God, saying, "Send out your light and your truth; let them lead me; let them bring me to your holy hill and to your dwelling! ⁴ Then I will go to the altar of God, to God my exceeding joy, and I will praise you with the lyre, O God, my God." This points out to us that no one can approach God or seek Him and find Him. Man can only find God when He—God—seeks man! This ends the search because man must admit that when man has access to God it is because God sought and found him—not vice versa.

When man seeks God on his own, the devil steps in to deceive and lead him astray. All searches for God end up in confusion and frustration. Until a person is born again having been sought by God, then and only then can he, *after* he is born again, seek God and draw near to Him. James 4:8 says, "Draw near to God, and He will draw near to you. Cleanse your hands, you sinners, and purify your hearts, you double-minded."

Accessibility to God comes only after a person is "cleaned up." In Psalm 24:3–5 King David says, "Who shall ascend the hill of the LORD? And who shall stand in his holy place? ⁴ He who has clean hands and a pure heart, who does not lift up his soul to what is false and does not swear deceitfully."

The main message is this: no one can have access to God unless he is cleaned up first!

Accessibility to God makes possible intimacy and closeness to God. In Psalm 27:4 King David says, "One thing have I asked of the LORD, that will I seek after: that I may dwell in the house of the LORD all the days of my life, to gaze upon the beauty of the LORD and to inquire in his temple." David's number one passion in life was to be in the presence of God continually. After a person has access to God and learns to "feast on God"—that is, to become totally satisfied with Him—then the driving passion of life is to stay in His presence continually. That is the greatest pleasure of the Christian's life. Now access is complete, and blessings flow from God to and through His people. In Psalm 65:4 David described the rich blessings of God this way: "Blessed is the one you choose and bring near, to dwell in your courts! We shall be satisfied with the goodness of your house, the holiness of your temple!"

Accessibility to God comes when we come in the proper way prepared by God for us. Psalm 145:18 and Isaiah 55:3 emphasize that when a person has access to God, then he needs to call on Him, yes, call on Him according to the way, the pathway, that He has made available to us. And it happens when we bend our ear, come to Him, and listen carefully. Then you will find out what real living is all about. When a person is cleaned up—born again, as Jesus called it—then he can begin to call out to God because he has come in the right way. There is great access for the believer who seeks God because he is seeking God in the one and only prescribed way God has made available to him.

Jesus is the great "Master Teacher on access" because He is the access to God. Jesus boldly said in John 14: I am the only way to God, the only truth about God, and the very life of God! No one can approach the Father except through Me! Paul tells us in 1 Timothy 2:5 says, "For there is one God, and there is one mediator between God and men, the man Christ Jesus." That is the authoritative word of the Son of God!

Many teach that the only way to God is through some human mediator, such as a priest or a holy man, but in the above verse we are assured that there is only one Mediator. At this point in the church age, we are encouraged to bring one another's needs to God in prayer, and we bring every need of our hearts to our advocate, Jesus Christ, the One who blazed a trail from earth to God's throne so that we could bring our needs to God and receive God's grace and power for each day (See Hebrews 4:16).

Other religions claim to be a pathway to God, but they are all dead-end roads that lead a person nowhere! Every religious leader claims to be a messiah or a guru or a great leader, but they all have one major fault—they died! That ends their claim! Jesus also claimed to be the Messiah, but He went on and proved that He is the only way to God and the author of eternal life when He did what no other religious leader did—He raised Himself from the dead!

Accessibility to God is not a public display. Jesus said to the disciples and the crowd in the Sermon on the Mount in Matthew 6:6–8: "But when you pray, go into your room and shut the door and pray to your

Father who is in secret. And your Father who sees in secret will reward you. [7] And when you pray, do not heap up empty phrases as the Gentiles do, for they think that they will be heard for their many words. [8] Do not be like them, for your Father knows what you need before you ask him." Jesus' point is this: Don't expect to be rewarded for what you do for God here on earth! When you pray or give or fast privately, then He will reward you in heaven, publicly!

Accessibility to God comes when we go through the "door," Jesus Christ. Twice in John 10, in verses 7 and 9, Jesus said, "I am the door." Not only is He the only door available to man for salvation, but He is the only door of access to the Father. He says that if we enter by Him, we will be eternally delivered from God's wrath and given eternal life and will go in and out through that door and become totally satisfied. The dissatisfaction in man's soul is acute and finds its fulfillment and answer only in access through Jesus Christ, our Lord and Savior! Where else could a believer find access and contentment?

Accessibility to God comes through faith. This is further explained by Paul in Acts 14:27. When Paul, a Jew, came to Antioch, Luke recorded this: "And when they arrived and gathered the church together, they declared all that God had done with them, and how he had opened a door of faith to the Gentiles." This greatly expands the idea of access. Was access available to only a few or to only one nation on earth? *No!* Now the "door of faith," the door of access to God through Jesus Christ, was made available to the Gentile world. Now all people everywhere, when they became believers, had access—unlimited access to the throne of God.

Paul amplifies this thought further in Romans 5:1–2 when he says, "Therefore, since we have been justified by faith, we have peace with God through our Lord Jesus Christ. [2] Through him we have also obtained access by faith into this grace in which we stand, and we rejoice in hope of the glory of God." Now we, too, the Gentiles and all believers everywhere, have open and unlimited access to God. Not only can we come, but we are now plugged into the "power of God" or the grace God gives us for each day because of that access.

Accessibility to God is open to all peoples on earth and brings them hope. Ephesians 2:12–22 informs us: "…remember that you were at that time separated from Christ, alienated from the commonwealth of Israel and strangers to the covenants of promise, having no hope and without God in the world. [13] But now in Christ Jesus you who once were far off have been brought near by the blood of Christ. [14] For he himself is our peace, who has made us both one and has broken down in his flesh the dividing wall of hostility [15] by abolishing the law of commandments expressed in ordinances, that he might create in himself one new man in place of the two, so making peace, [16] and might reconcile us both to God in one body through the cross, thereby killing the hostility. [17] And he came and preached peace to you who were far off and peace to those who were near. [18] For through him we both have access in one Spirit to the Father. [19] So then you are no longer strangers and aliens, but you are fellow citizens with the saints and members of the household of God, [20] built on the foundation of the apostles and prophets, Christ Jesus himself being the cornerstone, [21] in whom the whole structure, being joined together, grows into a holy temple in the Lord. [22] In him you also are being built together into a dwelling place for God by the Spirit."

This gives great hope to people who at one time felt far from God; now they can be drawn near because He paid the penalty for their sin, the very thing that put us at a distance from God. Taking that one step further, Ephesians 3:12 tells us the degree to which we have access. "…in whom we have boldness and access with confidence through our faith in him." Now not only do we have access, but we have it boldly and with confidence as we put our full faith and trust in Jesus Christ.

Hebrews 6:19–20 completes the thought by telling us: "We have this as a sure and steadfast anchor of the soul, a hope that enters into the inner place behind the curtain, [20] where Jesus has gone as a forerunner on our behalf, having become a high priest forever after the order of Melchizedek." What a great hope we have—Jesus blazed a trail from earth right into the throne room of God, and we can follow in His steps because we now have access to that throne! Hebrews 4:16 reaffirms this when the writer urges us: "Let us then with confidence draw near to the throne of grace, that we may receive mercy and find grace to help in time of need."

Accessibility to God means that reconciliation must take place. For reconciliation to take place, there must have been hostility between us and God. Yet He took the initiative to destroy the hostility and give us unlimited access to His throne. Colossians 1:19–22 tells us, "For in him all the fullness of God was pleased to dwell, [20] and through him to reconcile to himself all things, whether on earth or in heaven, making peace by the blood of his cross. [21] And you, who once were alienated and hostile in mind, doing evil deeds, [22] he has now reconciled in his body of flesh by his death, in order to present you holy and blameless and above reproach before him." That is great news because we were so far off and lost and hopeless, but now we have had the hostilities destroyed through Jesus Christ, and in Him we now have unlimited access to Almighty God!

Accessibility to God is possible because God reached down to the lowest sinner. Hebrews 7:25 emphasizes the ability of God in providing access to the most renegade among us. Is anyone hopeless? Is anyone too far away? What if I sin *after* I am born again—like many of the Bible characters did? The word is this: "Consequently, he is able to save to the uttermost those who draw near to God through him, since he always lives to make intercession for them." That gives peace of mind to all who desire access to God's throne. Jesus didn't just forgive and cleanse us from past sins; He took care of all our sins—past, present, and future. No one is hopeless. No one is too far away. All is based on these words: "He is able!"

Accessibility to God was framed in the Old Testament and completed in the New Testament. Hebrews 7:18–19 contrasts for us the old covenant with God and the new covenant. The old covenant was annulled and weak and worthless because it was only a pattern of what was to come. It says, "For on the one hand, a former commandment is set aside because of its weakness and uselessness [19] (for the law made nothing perfect); but on the other hand, a better hope is introduced, through which we draw near to God." What could the Old Testament sacrifices do to take away our sins and bring us near to God? Nothing! They were there so we could fully understand what Jesus did when He came. He took away "the weak" and gave us "the sure"! He took those who were farthest away from God and made it possible for all of us to "draw near"! Aren't you glad the old is past and gone?

Accessibility to God gives us boldness. To bolster our confidence even more, we are told in Hebrews 10:19–22, "Therefore, brothers, since we have confidence to enter the holy places by the blood of Jesus, [20] by the new and living way that he opened for us through the curtain, that is, through his flesh, [21] and since we have a great priest over the house of God, [22] let us draw near with a true heart in full assurance of faith, with our hearts sprinkled clean from an evil conscience and our bodies washed with pure water." Again the emphasis is on boldness because of what Jesus did for us!

Can accessibility to God make us a close friend of God's? A believer who desires to draw close to God can become as Abraham, who was called "the friend of God." Hebrews 11:6 gives us part of the answer when it explains that without faith it is impossible to please God. The one who comes to God must first believe that He exists and second that He rewards believers who diligently seek Him. God is ready and willing and available, but few believers seem to take the time and effort to make for themselves a diligent search of closeness with God. James 4:8 reminds us that when we "Draw near to God, and he will draw near to you. Cleanse your hands, you sinners, and purify your hearts, you double-minded." This will bring us into a close friendship with the eternal God.

Accessibility is complete when we call on God as our Father. Peter gives us a few final thoughts when he says, "Draw near to God, and he will draw near to you. Cleanse your hands, you sinners, and purify your hearts, you double-minded." (1 Peter 1:17). The Bible calls Him the Father to the fatherless. However and whenever our human father lets us down— and they always will—our heavenly Father steps in and completes the job no earthly father can do. Then Peter reiterates the reason Jesus had to suffer and die when he says in 1 Peter 2:18-19, "...knowing that you were ransomed from the futile ways inherited from your forefathers, not with perishable things such as silver or gold, [19] but with the precious blood of Christ, like that of a lamb without blemish or spot." The price was great, but for us it becomes the theme of our eternal song when we are reminded that it was for our sin, not His, for which He suffered an awful death; and He makes us alive by His Spirit!

Seek

When one looks at all of the character qualities and descriptive terms about God, it is easy to see that two-thirds of the references are in the Old Testament, and about one-third are in the New Testament. Two noteworthy examples are these: God as our Father and access to God. Why is that? We would never find much out about God as our Father until the Son showed up, and we found out how we can has access to God through His Son, Jesus Christ!

Since there is no access to the Father except through the Son (1 Timothy 2:5), accessibility to God is not spoken much about until the Son shows up. He is described like this in Hebrews 1:1–3: "Long ago, at many times and in many ways, God spoke to our fathers by the prophets, [2] but in these last days he has spoken to us by his Son, whom he appointed the heir of all things, through whom also he created the world. [3] He is the radiance of the glory of God and the exact imprint of his nature, and he upholds the universe by the word of his power. After making purification for sins, he sat down at the right hand of the Majesty on high." A good boss here on earth will make himself accessible to those he works with. God's design for access is so perfect because it brings us to seeking Him and then bowing in worship and praise. In the Old Testament they came to God, even before the actual access had been opened up—but they came, and so must we. So it turns out that access to God is summed up in the person of Jesus Christ. This means He is the only one qualified to open the door of access between sinful man and a holy God. And now, as born-again believers, we can use that access to have Him fill our hearts with the awe and wonder of praise and worship!

Worship

Pause to Praise and Worship: O God, where would each of us believers be if we didn't have full and unhindered access to You? If it weren't for access to You, we would easily be swallowed up by the world and never become overcomers! Thanks so much for opening the door for access to Your throne, the centcom of the universe. Now we can boldly come and receive the things we need most: the intimacy, the mercy, the grace, and the strength to live daily and be victorious because You have so graciously invited us to come to You. Forever we will worship You and enjoy coming often and kneeling before You in worship and praise. You indeed are awesome!

Chapter 8

Presence: Everywhere and Close By

Psalm 139:7: "Where shall I go from your Spirit? Or where shall I flee from your presence?"

- Can a person actually see the living God?
- What does He look like?
- Why can't everyone see Him?
- Does He, at times, appear as a man?
- What is man's reaction when he sees God?
- Is God right here all the time—we just can't see Him?
- How does His presence affect my life?

Many people claim they have seen an angel or some other angelic being, but can any human being actually see God and live to tell about it? The Bible tells us in John 4:24 that God is a Spirit, and you can't see a spirit being—that is, with our human eyes we have can't see the invisible. Yet many accounts come to us in the Bible that people "saw God" or "the angel of the Lord." How did they see God and live to tell the story?

Know

Who in the Scripture had the presence of God revealed to them? The list is long, but it includes Adam and Eve, Cain, Abraham and Sarah, Jacob,

Hagar, those who offered sacrifices to God, the Israelites in Egypt and as they were brought up out of bondage, and anyone who had a humble and contrite spirit. In short, His presence is not far from anyone.

One thing that helps us is this: God is not only present at times, but He is everywhere all the time. That is hard for us who are confined to a physical body to understand and comprehend. So, if God is here and God is everywhere, why can't we see Him all the time? Many times in our lives, we are aware of the presence of God (that is, those who are true believers, those who are born again spiritually), but we don't actually see Him with our physical eyes. Let's look first at some examples in Scripture of people who "met with God"—that is, God came to them appearing as a physical being like us—and then let's see how those who were "in the spirit," like Daniel and John, saw God and tried to describe what they saw when they were, in the spirit, taken into the throne room of God.

When Adam and Eve sinned in the Garden of Eden, it is recorded several times that God gave Adam a command. Later He said it wasn't good that man should be alone, so He created a woman—one to complete and complement Adam. Did God appear in a physical body to them, and later to Cain when he brought a sacrifice to God and God spoke to him? The answer is in Genesis 3:8 where it says, "And they heard the sound of the LORD God walking in the garden in the cool of the day, and the man and his wife hid themselves from the presence of the LORD God among the trees of the garden." It is never stated here that God appeared to them in a physical body (though He could have), but He did speak directly to them, in an audible voice, and they knew He was there and could see them because, after they had sinned, they made coverings of fig leaves for themselves and hid from His presence. So, at this point in history, God spoke to them using an audible voice, they knew He was there, and yet they didn't see Him.

Occurrences like these are many in the Old Testament. God spoke to Moses, Abraham, Isaac, Jacob, and many others, but it seems from the record that they heard His voice but did not see His form. People who actually heard God's voice describe it as like the sound of thunder. Job 37:2–5 tells us to listen attentively to the thunder of God's voice as it rumbles from His mouth. He sends the lightning and thunder all over the earth. It is like a giant roar, the sound of a majestic voice that is not restrained. God's voice thunders with a deep resonating boom, and no one can comprehend what He is doing. So, when we hear thunder, think of it as being like the voice of Almighty God when He speaks. In Psalm 29 we have a further description of the power of God's voice. It says the voice of the Lord is powerful and majestic. With His voice He breaks cedar trees, cuts through flames of fire, shakes the deserts, makes deer to calve, strips the forest till it is bare, yet sits as King over the floods! And He does all of this with His majestic voice. When God chooses to speak audibly, it is in a powerful booming voice; yet when He speaks to a believer, He can speak in a "still small voice", an inner voice, like He did to Elijah in the cave (see I Kings 19:11-12). The main point here is this: when we hear the voice of God, we know that His presence is near. Isn't this one of the ways that God reassures us with His presence?

God's presence came to Hagar when she met the angel of the Lord. Genesis 16:7–13 gives us the story of Hagar when she fled from Sarah. The record says several times that "the angel of the LORD" appeared to her. This is what is referred to by theologians as "christophanies," or Old Testament appearances of Christ. Here, and elsewhere, are times when a visible representation of God came, and He is specifically here referred to as "the angel of the Lord." Hagar makes an interesting observation in verse 13 when she makes the statement and asks the rhetorical question when she called the name of the Lord who spoke to her, "You are the God who sees me," and she also asked, "Have I actually seen the God who sees me?" She was aware that she had seen a visible representation of God—or God Himself—and more than that, she was aware that He is always there, "seeing me." We too should be aware that even though we can't always see God or feel His presence, He is always there, and He sees us and all we do and say!

God's presence came to Jacob in a dream. When Jacob left home because of his brother's death threat, he camped one night near Bethel and had a dream. In the vision he saw a ladder from earth to heaven, and angels of God were walking up and down on this giant staircase, and the Lord stood above it and spoke to him and reaffirmed the promise He had made to Abraham and Isaac concerning this land and "in your descendant all nations of the earth will be blessed" (Genesis 28:10–16). When Jacob woke up, he said, "Surely the Lord is in this place; and I did not know it." Then he continued and made a vow to God. Jacob was in a time of deep distress and crisis when God met him. Jacob was aware that God came and spoke specifically to him, and he was assured from that point on in his life that God was with him and protected him and blessed him greatly.

Isn't that what God does when He comes to us? Yes, we are afraid, like Jacob, but we know that we have met with Almighty God, that His angels are there constantly ministering to us, and that He will work all things out in our lives to fulfill His promise to us and to bless us exceedingly. That is encouraging!

Later in Jacob's life, when he was returning from Mesopotamia, it is recorded in Genesis 32:24–32 that Jacob wrestled with a man until the next day dawned. As he wrestled with this "man," Jacob began to realize that he was wrestling with God. Jacob had hold of Him and refused to let go until He blessed him. This was another "christophany" or a visit by "the angel of the LORD," but it brings out an interesting point. God has the ability to reveal Himself or to appear in different forms, each one veiling the brilliance of His glory and majesty and splendor. So, yes, God can appear as a man, an angel, or in any form He chooses. He later appeared to Abraham as a Man walking down the dusty trail; He appeared to Jacob as a Man with whom Jacob wrestled; and He appeared to Saul of Tarsus as "a brilliant blinding light."

God's presence comes with a warning. God sternly warned man not to make a physical representation of God as a visible sign of His presence. Exodus 20:22–24 tells us one of the important functions of an altar. Here's what it says, "And the LORD said to Moses, 'Thus you shall say to the people of Israel: "You have seen for yourselves that I have talked with you from heaven. 23 You shall not make gods of silver to be with me, nor shall you make for yourselves gods of gold. 24 An altar of earth you shall make for me and sacrifice on it your burnt offerings and your peace offerings, your sheep and your oxen. In every place where I cause my name to be remembered I will come to you and bless you." '"

Whenever we make an acceptable sacrifice that God asks of us, He then promises that He will meet us there and bless us. So the presence of God and the blessings from God come together. The point is this: whenever we too make an acceptable sacrifice to God, He comes to meet with us and bless us and manifest His presence to us like He promised to do for Israel when they built an altar.

God's presence shocks the world around us! What is the response of the world around us when God makes His presence known? Joshua 2:8–11 recounts the story of Rahab, an inhabitant of Jericho, when Israel came to attack the city. She said, "Before the men lay down, she came up to them on the roof[9] and said to the men, 'I know that the LORD has given you the land, and that the fear of you has fallen upon us, and that all the inhabitants of the land melt away before you. [10] For we have heard how the LORD dried up the water of the Red Sea before you when you came out of Egypt, and what you did to the two kings of the Amorites who were beyond the Jordan, to Sihon and Og, whom you devoted to destruction. [11] And as soon as we heard it, our hearts melted, and there was no spirit left in any man because of you, for the LORD your God, he is God in the heavens above and on the earth beneath." Wow! Since God's presence is always with His saints, wherever believers go, God is with them, and when the world sees God do great things in and through us, their hearts also melt for fear. That's why we can go forth in His name confidently.

God's presence is manifested exclusively to and through His children. When God's presence is manifested, it assures us that He is the only God. Listen to what God said through Moses as Israel was about to enter the Promised Land in Deuteronomy 4:33–39: "Did any people ever hear the voice of a god speaking out of the midst of the fire, as you have heard, and still live? [34] Or has any god ever attempted to go and take a nation for himself from the midst of another nation, by trials, by signs, by wonders, and by war, by a mighty hand and an outstretched arm, and by great deeds of terror, all of which the LORD your God did for you in Egypt before your eyes? [35] To you it was shown, that you might know that the LORD is God; there is no other besides him. [36] Out of heaven he let you hear his voice, that he might discipline you. And on earth he let you see his great fire, and you heard his words out of the midst of the fire. [37] And because he loved your fathers and chose their offspring after them and brought you out of Egypt with his own presence, by his great power, [38] driving out before you nations greater and mightier than you, to bring you in, to give you their land for an inheritance, as it is this day, [39] know therefore today, and lay it to your heart, that the LORD is God in heaven above and on the earth beneath; there is no other."

It gives us great comfort to know that as God's presence was with them, so He will always be with us. He spoke to them out of the fire, He performed signs that showed strength and power, and all of this to show His love to them and prove to the world around them that He is God and there is none other!

One thought that challenges the mind is this: In this passage God's presence, His voice, and fire are mentioned together. Recently it was discovered through experimentation that a voice is greatly amplified when it comes out of a fire. At times in the Scripture when the throne of God is seen and described, it says that there were lightnings and thunderings and voices: and there were seven lamps of fire burning before the throne (for example: Revelation 4:5). Those who witnessed the giving of the law on Mount Sinai also saw lighting, thunder, and fire come from the mountain as God revealed His presence to Moses and spoke audibly to them. God has many ways of making Himself known and heard.

God's presence brings reassurance. When God's presence is felt, it reassures us that His hand is on our lives. King David said in Psalm 139:5, "Thou hast beset me behind and before, and laid thine hand upon me." David was saying that God is all around us. He surrounds us. David felt God's presence "hedge him in." This is what brings peace and confidence to a believer's life.

What characteristics of a man invite the presence of God? When God in heaven looks down on earth, what kind of person is He looking to show His presence to? Isaiah 57:15 answers by saying, "For thus says the One who is high and lifted up, who inhabits eternity, whose name is Holy: 'I dwell in the high and holy place, and also with him who is of a contrite and lowly spirit, to revive the spirit of the lowly, and to revive the heart of the contrite.'" Isaiah 66:1–2 adds this thought: God will look on the person who is poor and has a contrite spirit and *who trembles at God's Word*. God has chosen to work through people on earth who have a humble spirit, a contrite heart, and who tremble at His words. Then His presence will be known through those people to the rest of the world around them! Another important point from this passage: God's presence is especially close to His holy children. God loves to manifest His presence to and through His special chosen ones.

Can a person get away from God's presence? Listen to King David's words in Psalm 139:7–12, as he describes the awesome, inescapable presence of God: "Where shall I go from your Spirit? Or where shall I flee from your presence? [8] If I ascend to heaven, you are there! If I make my bed in Sheol, you are there! [9] If I take the wings of the morning and dwell in the uttermost parts of the sea, [10] even there your hand shall lead me, and your right hand shall hold me. [11] If I say, 'Surely the darkness shall cover me, and the light about me be night,' [12] even the darkness is not dark to you; the night is bright as the day, for darkness is as light with you." These words of reassurance come to people who are alone or feel like they are all by themselves when going through difficult times. For sure God wants us to go through many deep waters with no other human being to help us, but He *always* reassures us of His presence as we go through troubled times!

Jeremiah 23:23–24 reaffirms these words when he says, "Am I a God at hand, declares the LORD, and not a God far away? [24] Can a man hide himself in secret places so that I cannot see him? declares the LORD. Do I not fill heaven and earth? declares the LORD." The fact is this: you couldn't get away from God if you wanted to! Ephesians 1:23 also tells us that God fills the whole universe, which is a character quality of God known as ubiquitous. What an awesome thought!

Flee from God's presence? One of God's prophets, Jonah, mistakenly thought he could flee away from God's presence and then not have to go to those evil people in Nineveh with the gospel of repentance. Jonah 1:3–4 tell us that after the LORD had come to Jonah and told him to go to Nineveh, we are told Jonah got up and took off running to Tarshish (the opposite direction from Nineveh) in order to flee from the presence of the Lord. How far did he get? The LORD sent out a strong violent wind on the Mediterranean Sea, and the waves and wind were so violent the ship began to break up. He found out fast that you cannot get away from the presence of the LORD.

Later, after Jonah had been thrown overboard (at his own request), it says Jonah 2:1–3: "Then Jonah prayed to the LORD his God from the belly of the fish, ² saying, 'I called out to the LORD, out of my distress, and he answered me; out of the belly of Sheol I cried, and you heard my voice. ³ For you cast me into the deep, into the heart of the seas, and the flood surrounded me; all your waves and your billows passed over me." One reason this story is in the Scriptures is to let us know that God's presence is everywhere and no man can escape from it, and that we can pray to God to help us no matter what dire circumstances we are in, or no matter where we are.

God's presence helps us communicate hope. As we live in a world where most people around us are unbelievers who are lost, how do we communicate the hope that we have to them? Acts 17:26–28 says, "And he made from one man every nation of mankind to live on all the face of the earth, having determined allotted periods and the boundaries of their dwelling place, ²⁷ that they should seek God, and perhaps feel their way toward him and find him. Yet he is actually not far from each one of us, ²⁸ for 'In him we live and move and have our being'; as even some of your own poets have said, 'For we are indeed his offspring.'" We can confidently tell a lost world that He is near, and that can give them hope that one day they will know Him and His presence will be felt in their lives!

Seek

How does the presence of God touch us in a practical daily way? One problem we face often is grappling with fear. One of the great promises of the Bible will help us conclude this section: Don't let fear grab hold of you, because God is with you. How many times did God say that in Scripture? Someone has counted and said that this promise is repeated to many different people and groups of people hundreds of times! Is anything more reassuring to a believer than this great promise? "Fear not, for I am with you!" For the believer God's presence takes fear out! This is why the presence of God is spoken of so often in the Bible. God has designed this world for us so that we can't see Him with physical eyes, but with the eyes of our spirit, we can see Him and know Him daily, and His presence takes the fear, the dread, and the sheer terror of our enemy out of our lives.

As we have looked at the presence of God throughout the Bible, it strikes us that since He revealed Himself to many in the Scriptures, He also can and will reveal Himself to us on a daily basis. Many who have gone through a traumatic time in their life—whether a distressing trial, a serious illness, or a near-death experience—have come out of that difficulty with an awareness of the presence of God like never before. They have been deeply reassured of His presence, and as David said in Psalm 23 that even though we go through the valley of the shadow of death, God is with us all the way. It is extremely valuable to any believer to walk each day with the consciousness of His presence since it gives us hope, comfort, and encouragement as we walk hand in hand with our Savior. The stories in the Bible don't seem so far off and strange anymore because the same thing has happened to us that happened to the Bible characters, and it is His presence we long to live in forever as we spend eternity in His presence. I believe this is one of the main reasons God puts us through those trials and afflictions—to know firsthand His presence.

One critical closing thought of encouragement: God's presence and His Word go together. The two cannot be separated. Since God has chosen to reveal Himself through word descriptions of Himself, we must seek His presence often in His Word, the Bible. We must find huge chunks of time to spend in the Word, reading, studying, memorizing, and meditating on it, if we are to experience His presence in a meaningful way. You will never feel the presence of God in your life on a continuing basis unless you make the Word of God the number one priority in your life.

Worship

Pause to Praise and Worship: O God, as we bow our hearts before You, we are aware every time we pray of Your presence that You have made possible for us to enjoy. Our hearts are caught up in praise and worship whenever we bow at Your feet in prayer. To commune with You is the greatest privilege any man on earth can experience, so we come. We come often; we come closer. In fact, as we seek You, we thrive on that greatest feeling of any person on earth—the closeness and the intimacy of Your presence. We bow in worship of You!

Chapter 9

Righteous: High Standard but Available to All

Romans 1:17: "For in it the righteousness of God is revealed from faith for faith, as it is written, 'The righteous shall live by faith.'"

- What does it mean to be righteous?
- Who sets the standard as to what is right and what is wrong?
- What is the righteousness of God based on?
- Is anyone born a "righteous" or a good person?
- How does a sinful person get the righteousness of God?
- Where does the righteousness of God ultimately lead us?

One characteristic of man from the beginning of creation is that he tries in many different ways to define what is right and what is wrong. When we accept the truth from Scripture that man is born a sinner and that we are all sinners since Adam and Eve sinned in the Garden of Eden, it would be easy to then conclude that no one is a righteous person and no one can become a righteous person. What man *must do* is step aside and let his Creator define righteousness, describe it, and then tell us how to get it, what happens if we don't have it, and where a sinner is ultimately headed when he is clothed in God's perfect righteousness.

Know

Let's start at the beginning: What is righteousness? Does the Bible declare that God is righteous? "God is righteous" is the declaration in Ezra 9:15; Psalm 7:9; 11:7; 50:6; 71:15, 19; Jeremiah 12:1; Daniel 9:7, 14; John 17:25; and Revelation 16:5. So righteousness starts in the character of God—the essence of who He is. To be righteous is to be good, holy, without sin, and is laid alongside His justice and judgment (because God's justice and judgment come from the quality of His being righteous). In a court of law, we are always looking for what is truth, what is right, and what are the facts. Then a decision can be made according to the laws in force at the time in question. In God's supreme court in heaven, everything is evaluated and judged according to His character—what He calls good, holy, and just—and His character doesn't change and cannot be trumped.

In Psalm 11:7, the focus is on God's character. It says, "For the LORD is righteous; he loves righteous deeds; the upright shall behold his face." Here we are told that the LORD is righteous, He loves righteousness, and His countenance beams when he sees men living right. So not only is He righteous, but He has a great passion for promoting His righteousness, and it pleases Him well when we demonstrate it on a daily basis. The bottom line is this: when speaking about the righteousness of God, it is the founding principles, the basic law by which all people will be judged; it is the foundation of His character. Therefore, righteousness must be outlined, revealed, instituted, and carried out only by God alone, and He delights when He sees it in us!

Let's let the Word speak for itself as we look at the various passages that speak about righteousness.

God's righteous character is our ultimate standard to live by. Ezra 9:15 says this: "O LORD, the God of Israel, you are just, for we are left a remnant that has escaped, as it is today. Behold, we are before you in our guilt, for none can stand before you because of this." Ezra acknowledged that the judgment of God had come on Israel because of their great sin. Now many people had been wiped out, and only a few remained—and they determined to live right before God. When Ezra and his contemporaries saw the judgment of God on Israel for their idolatry and their rebellion against God's laws, it was clear to them what God's righteousness was.

God's righteousness is seen clearly when one looks at man's ineptness in handling life. As man looks at other men and in the mirror at himself, he is constantly reminded of man's fragility, weakness, and sinful condition. Elihu, one of Job's friends, said in essence Job 36:3, "I will get my knowledge from afar and ascribe righteousness to my Maker." Man's best attempts at setting up laws to govern and deciding what is right and what is wrong are at best weak; so we must get our cue for what is right and what is wrong from our Maker—He made everything and established all the rules in the game of life.

In Psalm 50:6, Asaph tells us, "The heavens declare his righteousness, for God himself is judge! *Selah*" Here we find that the whole universe tells us about His righteousness—because God Himself is the ultimate Judge. When man looks at the decisions of politicians and judges and others in government and sees their flaws, he rejoices when he sees the good and righteous decisions God hands down.

God's righteousness must be shown on a continual basis. David in Psalm 5:8 says, "Lead me, O LORD, in your righteousness because of my enemies; make your way straight before me." He goes on in Psalm 7:9 to say, "Oh, let the evil of the wicked come to an end, and may you establish the righteous—you who test the minds and hearts, O righteous God!" The way of the wicked people on earth must be continually exposed, and the way of the righteous people needs to be lifted up continually, and then God's *righteous* character will be clearly seen.

Why are God's righteousness and justice inseparable? They are inseparable chiefly because God's righteousness becomes the basis of all of God's judicial decisions. In David's psalm to the soon-to-be king, Solomon (Psalm 72:1), David asks God to give Solomon His judgments and to show to Solomon His righteousness, and then he goes on to explain that he will need it in judging the people. Any nation (Israel or modern America) that has their laws firmly centered on God's determination of what is right and wrong will need her leaders to see God's judicial decisions that are handed down and to judge their people accordingly.

Ethan, the follower of Ezra the scribe, said in Psalm 89:14 that righteousness and justice are the foundation stones of God's throne; and when these two are administered, mercy and accuracy must also be taken into account (see also Psalm 97:2). Psalm 119:137 adds to this thought by saying, "Righteous are you, O LORD, and right are your rules." David continues the thought in Psalm 9:4, 8 by saying, "For you have maintained my just cause; you have sat on the throne, giving righteous judgment. . .and he judges the world with righteousness; he judges the peoples with uprightness." Acts 17:31 concludes this with the statement: "because he has fixed a day on which he will judge the world in righteousness by a man whom he has appointed; and of this he has given assurance to all by raising him from the dead." What would it be like to live in a world where man took God's righteousness as the standard, the basis, of all their laws?

What is the reaction of the world around us when they see God's righteousness held up high? Where, in our world and in our time, do we see these righteous decisions handed down by God? Psalm 88:12 asks that question: "Are your wonders known in the darkness, or your righteousness in the land of forgetfulness?" He is asking God, will Your fantastic deeds be obscure or Your righteousness in a place where people constantly forget things? Psalm 112:4 says, "Light dawns in the darkness for the upright; he is gracious, merciful, and righteous." For the morally upright person, light will be turned on in darkness because the LORD is gracious, has an abundant supply of compassion for man, yet He is righteous. When God's righteousness is seen, it turns on the lights, exposes darkness, and causes the righteous to once again rejoice! Watch how God deals with individuals and nations, and watch how they do things and accept things as if a driving force is behind them. They do things they never thought they would do. This is God at work in our world.

Do God's righteous standards change? People will say, "But you are talking about things that happened many years ago. These things don't apply to us now in a more intelligent and enlightened world." But God's righteous standards never change; they were made to last forever because they are based on the eternal unchanging character of God. Psalm 111:3 says, "Full of splendor and majesty is his work, and his righteousness endures forever." The Lord's work is honorable, glorious, and His righteousness will last forever. Man changes as the depth of the wickedness of man's heart is exposed, but since God doesn't and cannot change, neither will His standards for what is right and wrong.

What other character qualities of God are mentioned alongside His righteousness? One inescapable fact when studying the character of God is the way other characteristics, character qualities, attributes, or other word descriptions are used alongside each one. For example, when you look at God's righteousness, or the fact that He is righteous, you also find that His justice and judgment are mentioned. And His mercy, the fact that He is gracious, full of compassion, etc., is also brought to light. When you look at the rigid righteous standards of God' Laws, one could despair; but when you see that God is not only righteous but also merciful and full of compassion, it gives us hope and makes us seek His mercy.

Does God always act according to His righteous character? Psalm 145:17 says, "The LORD is righteous in all his ways and kind in all his works." So this points out the fact that the LORD is righteous in *all* He does. How could God act outside His eternal unchanging character? Only man can be good at one time and act in evil at other times. How could God be anything but righteous? He is righteous in everything He does because it is part of His eternal character.

Here are a few things that tell us what God's righteousness does for us:

1. Psalm 119:40 tells us that His righteousness revives me.

2. The psalmist pleads with God in 144:11 not only to revive me but to bring me out of trouble with God's righteousness. When my heart is faint and weary, it can and will be revived by seeing His righteousness.

3. Psalm 119:144 reaffirms to us that *all* of God's commandments are righteous. We can't pick and choose which ones we think are right or wrong; all are equally accurate and absolute.

4. In Isaiah 51:1–8, God's righteousness is described as it relates to the first man the Bible recorded that became righteous before God by faith. It also explains the duration of God's righteousness and who is to live under it. Listen to a few words from these verses:

"Listen to me, you who pursue righteousness, you who seek the LORD: look to the rock from which you were hewn, and to the quarry from which you were dug. ²Look to Abraham your father and to Sarah who bore you; for he was but one when I called him, that I might bless him and multiply him.³ For the LORD comforts Zion; he comforts all her waste places and makes her wilderness like Eden, her desert like the garden of the LORD; joy and gladness will be found in her, thanksgiving and the voice of song. ⁴Give attention to me, my people, and give ear to me, my nation; for a law will go out from me, and I will set my justice for a light to the peoples. ⁵My righteousness draws near, my salvation has gone out, and my arms will judge the peoples; the coastlands hope for me, and for my arm they wait. ⁶Lift up your eyes to the heavens, and look at the earth beneath; for the heavens vanish like smoke, the earth will wear out like a garment, and they who dwell in it will die in like manner; but my salvation will be forever, and my righteousness will never be dismayed. ⁷Listen to me, you who know righteousness, the people in whose heart is my law; fear not the reproach of man, nor be dismayed at their revilings. ⁸For the moth will eat them up like a garment, and the worm will eat them like wool, but my righteousness will be forever, and my salvation to all generations."

What happens when we make God's righteous character ours? As we study each word that describes God, many of these qualities we are to take and make them part of our lives. Two of these qualities are mentioned together in Isaiah 56:1: "Thus says the LORD: 'Keep justice, and do righteousness, for soon my salvation will come, and my righteousness be revealed.'" Of course, the fulfillment of this happened when Jesus Christ came to earth because He personified God's righteousness and made it available to us through the gospel. But the point to be made here is that, if justice is to be demonstrated on earth, it will come through believers; and if the world is to know anything about the righteous character of God, we must model it! This world will never know anything about the righteous character of God or what real justice is unless we demonstrate it to them. What an assignment we have!

Is boasting about God's righteousness ever right? Jeremiah 9:23–24 says, "Thus says the LORD: 'Let not the wise man boast in his wisdom, let not the mighty man boast in his might, let not the rich man boast in his riches, [24] but let him who boasts boast in this, that he understands and knows me, that I am the LORD who practices steadfast love, justice, and righteousness in the earth. For in these things I delight, declares the LORD." The believer who understands God's righteous character and speaks about it to others may be the only real witness some people will ever hear about Him—so speak up and brag on God! God is righteous; man is a sinner. One stark contrast in Scripture is this: God's righteous character is laid alongside man's failure and sin. Daniel 9:7, 14 says in part, "To you, O Lord, belongs righteousness, but to us open shame. . .for the LORD our God is righteous in all the works that he has done:" Our lives are filled with shame and embarrassment when we see the contrast of His perfect righteous character.

How do we get God's righteous character into our own lives? Paul explains in Romans how we can get God's righteousness—so much so that one day when we stand before Almighty God (who alone is holy and just) it will be determined that we too are standing there clothed in His righteous character. In Romans 1:17, Paul tells us that the righteousness of God is revealed in the gospel. That means that through the gospel and by God's grace through the gospel changing our lives, we too can receive His righteousness.

Later in Romans 3:21–22, Paul explains that the righteous character of God is revealed through the Law of Moses and also that it comes to us by grace through faith in Jesus Christ alone. Since it is by grace, we can't earn it, qualify for it, or obtain it by being born into a Christian home. In that same chapter in verses 25–26, we are told that God was completely satisfied with the sacrifice of Jesus on the cross because He lived a sinless life. All the sins of the past life are gone, and now He has declared us to be righteous; He can be just in declaring us righteous as we prepare to stand before Him.

This is the righteousness of God getting right down to where we are and putting His righteous clothes on us and into man's heart. Man has for centuries tried to set his own standard of what is right and wrong, but this is the only standard acceptable to God. Romans 10:3–4 informs us that God's righteous laws are after us, tracking us down, but the righteous demands of a perfect law stopped when it came to Christ—who became the curse for us. Jesus took all of our sins on Himself, and as 2 Corinthians 5:21 completes the thought when Paul said that God poured His righteousness into us! Second Peter 1:1 concludes by saying that we have obtained the most precious faith imaginable when we received the righteousness of God through Jesus Christ our Savior. That's true!

How does God's righteous character complete our life while here on earth? The challenge is put to us by our Lord when, in Matthew 6:33, we are told to seek first God's kingdom—and His righteousness—and all the temporal things of earth will be tacked on as a benefit to us. How much of our lives would be changed if we modeled His righteous character? How much of our anxiety would be gone if we had the proper perspective on earthly things and instead focused our attention on bringing about His righteousness?

What is the believer's ultimate end in eternity? Will we be modeling God's righteousness reigning supreme over His universe? When all of history is over on earth, we are told that we will be clothed in fine linen, white and clean, following our Lord. Then we will stand before God, not clothed in the filthy rags that we now wear but clothed in His righteousness. Second Timothy 4:8 tells us: "Henceforth there is laid up for me the crown of righteousness, which the Lord, the righteous judge, will award to me on that day, and not only to me but also to all who have loved his appearing."

That takes the righteousness of God full circle: it started in His character, was made available to those who put their trust in Him as their Savior, and then those believers will be clothed, not in those old filthy rags that we used to wear, but in His righteousness—ready to stand before Him forever and give praise and glory and honor to His name!

Seek

Now let's get down to earth and practical about how to express God's righteous character into our lives. Of course, it starts with having been given the righteousness of God at the time of salvation, but what happens after that?

On what basis can the heart of the righteous person sing praise to God? David records one way in Psalm 48:10–14, "As your name, O God, so your praise reaches to the ends of the earth. Your right hand is filled with righteousness. [11] Let Mount Zion be glad! Let the daughters of Judah rejoice because of your judgments! [12] Walk about Zion, go around her, number her towers, [13] consider well her ramparts, go through her citadels, that you may tell the next generation [14] that this is God, our God forever and ever. He will guide us forever." David pointed out that God's righteous character ignites the praise of us, His followers, and that through His righteousness we are guide throughout life.

In Psalm 71:15–19, the psalmist says: "My mouth will tell of your righteous acts, of your deeds of salvation all the day, for their number is past my knowledge. [16] With the mighty deeds of the Lord GOD I will come; I will remind them of your righteousness, yours alone. [17] O God, from my youth you have taught me, and I still proclaim your wondrous deeds. [18] So even to old age and gray hairs, O God, do not forsake me, until I proclaim your might to another generation, your power to all those to come. [19] Your righteousness, O God, reaches the high heavens. You who have done great things, O God, who is like you?"

Is God's righteousness some far-off concept we hope someday to witness? Will we ever see our sinful past and present lives put behind us forever and see the righteousness of God exalted? Listen to these words from Isaiah 46:12–13: "Listen to me, you stubborn of heart, you who are far from righteousness: [13] I bring near my righteousness; it is not far off, and my salvation will not delay; I will put salvation in Zion, for Israel my glory." Our hearts are all stubborn, hardened, and calloused, but God will cause His righteousness to prevail—even though many men will lose out and reject Him.

God's righteous character ignites praise in man's heart. Psalm 89:16 says that the people who know real joy in God's name will rejoice all day long, and when God's righteousness is upheld, those people will be exalted. Will it be known worldwide when a nation or a people uses God's righteousness as their standard? Yes, because that nation will be exalted as long as they hold to His righteous standard.

Psalm 7:17 adds to these thoughts by saying, "I will give to the LORD the thanks due to his righteousness, and I will sing praise to the name of the LORD, the Most High." What would it be like to live in a world where

God's righteousness reigns supreme? Of course we will know during the millennium, but Proverbs 11:10 tells us that when it goes well with the righteous, the whole city rejoices. There are glimpses of righteousness in our world, but for now we must be patient and wait—the day will come when, we, the righteous, will be ruling and reigning with Him. We will see His righteous character exalted, and it will make our hearts rejoice.

The righteous character of God needs to be the foundation of all justice and laws that are written. Man's system of laws will all fail because they are flawed and based on "the best man can do," but they fall far short of God's standard. God's standard of righteousness was revealed in the Mosaic Law. Man seeks to establish his own ideas of what is right and wrong and in doing so invites the judgment of God. This gives us insight into why God must eventually judge every man. We can be deceived and self-deceived so much that we miss seeing the pure, righteous character of God. When man turns from the Scriptures, he immediately is set up for judgment, but when we base our lives on God's righteousness revealed through and given by His Son, then and only then will we begin to understand God's righteousness.

Worship

Pause to Praise and Worship: O God, You have clearly revealed in Your Word what Your righteous standard is and how man can obtain Your righteousness by faith. Thank You for sending Your Son and through Him revealing the answer to Your laws and commands. It warms our hearts to see how we too can obtain Your righteous character by faith in Your Son, and we look forward to the day when we will stand before You dressed in Your righteousness. Thanks for opening that door for us.

Chapter 10

Wisdom: Only One True Source

Job 12:13 says of the Lord: "With God are wisdom and might; he has counsel and understanding."

- Who is wise?
- What is wisdom?
- What is the source of all wisdom, understanding, and knowledge?
- Isn't man getting smarter and smarter, and someday will he know "everything"?
- Is there wisdom that is beyond the reach of mortal man?
- How do we tap into God's wisdom?
- What are we to do with this "wisdom" once we get it?

Wisdom—what is it? Wisdom is more than accumulated knowledge or scientific learning; it goes beyond that and applies that knowledge and understanding in a practical way. A person can have a brilliant mind and be intelligent, but if he lives a sloppy, careless life, we say he is not very wise—he hasn't learned how to take all he knows and get breadth of understanding about life.

Know

In each word study on God's character, we must go to His Word, the Bible, for our information and definition. Let's start with one of the oldest books of the Bible—Job.

Think of all the knowledge and scientific understanding available in the universe, all it took to make the universe. God alone has it at His disposal, yet to take that vast, infinite body of knowledge and have a purpose in using it to create this world and man and all the intricacies in our world—now that takes an infinite amount of wisdom. In both Job 9:4 and 12:13, Job tells us that God is wise in heart and mighty in strength—who can stand against Him? And with God is both wisdom and strength; He owns both counsel and understanding! If you had all of the strength (or knowledge) in the universe at your fingertips, how could you use it wisely? Only God has all the strength, knowledge, and know-how to put it together in creating a world like ours.

This is one of the great examples of how to use wisdom: God has an infinite amount of wisdom, knowledge, and understanding, and He put it to use in making such a magnificent world for us to live in. So when we learn knowledge, wisdom, and understanding, we too must learn how to put that knowledge to use in our daily lives. For example, when God tells us sin enslaves and chains us, we can use that knowledge to stay away from sin, seek to have it cleansed from our lives, and never let it entangle us in its web. This is wisdom in action!

Another example is in the areas of finance. God gives us a number of basic principles of finance that work, and when we ignore them, we get into trouble and financial bondage. When we take those financial principles and put them into our personal daily lives, then we can have the peace and freedom that comes with them—and that is wisdom, taking from the Bible knowledge that helps our daily lives and just following the instructions given to us. For example, if the financial principles America received from the Bible are ever taken out from our nation, it will collapse financially!

Does God give His wisdom to man when he needs it most? The story in the following verses chronicles the predicament Daniel and his three friends found themselves in. The king had demanded that they tell him not only the interpretation of his dream that night, but they were also to tell him the dream! Now that is unreasonable. God then answered their prayer and revealed both the dream and the interpretation to Daniel, and in his prayer of thanksgiving to God after God had revealed the king's dream to him, Daniel said in 2:20–23, "Daniel answered and said: 'Blessed be the name of God forever and ever, to whom belong wisdom and might. [21] He changes times and seasons; Daniel answered and said: 'Blessed be the name of God forever and ever, to whom belong wisdom and might. [21] He changes times and seasons; he removes kings and sets up kings; he gives wisdom to the wise and knowledge to those who have understanding; [22] he reveals deep and hidden things; he knows what is in the darkness, and the light dwells with him. [23] To you, O God of my fathers, I give thanks and praise, for you have given me wisdom and might, and have now made known to me what we asked of you, for you have made known to us the king's matter.'"

So God not only has wisdom—all wisdom—but He also gives it to His children when they need it most! Later Daniel would say to King Nebuchadnezzar in verse 28, "…but there is a God in heaven who reveals mysteries, and he has made known to King Nebuchadnezzar what will be in the latter days. Your dream and the visions of your head as you lay in bed are these:" Daniel made sure to attribute all wisdom and power to God and to Him alone. In Romans 16:27, the apostle Paul repeated this same thought when he said, "To the God only wise . . ." And in 1 Timothy 1:17, Paul again states in a benediction: "To the King of the ages, immortal, invisible, the only God, be honor and glory forever and ever. Amen." These verses prove to us that all wisdom comes from God and Him alone and that His wisdom is available to His children when they need it.

God's wisdom is vast. In Psalm 104:24, the writer says, "O LORD, how manifold are your works! In wisdom have you made them all; the earth is full of your creatures." The more science looks at what man can feel, touch, and explore here on earth, the more evident it becomes that there are vast quantities of treasures yet to be discovered. Psalm 136:5 gives praise to God, saying, "to him who by understanding made the heavens," Can you imagine the vast amount of knowledge it took to create this universe—and each tiny flower and bug on earth? But to put everything together so that it works harmoniously is far beyond our comprehension! Jeremiah 10:12 and 51:15 say to us in unison that God has handmade the earth by His awesome power, established the world by His infinite wisdom, and, at His discretion and understanding, He merely stretched out the universe.

Proverbs 3:19–20 follows up this thought proclaiming, "The LORD by wisdom founded the earth; by understanding he established the heavens; [20] by his knowledge the deeps broke open, and the clouds drop down the dew." So the LORD, using His vast supply of wisdom, brought this earth into existence; and with His vast supply of understanding, He set the universe in motion. Using His knowledge He moves the crust of the earth (as in Noah's flood), and makes clouds drop down the dew to water the earth.

The book of Proverbs was written to help all of us who have a foolish heart become wise. Chapter 8 is especially rich because God speaks, as though wisdom itself was speaking, and gives advice to us. Here are a few of the words from that chapter, written in a paraphrase, as God's wisdom speaks, beckoning us to learn wisdom from God and become wise: Can't you hear wisdom crying out? Doesn't understanding speak loud and clear to you? She (wisdom) is standing on the rooftop, calling out to those passing by. She cries out in the halls of government, city council meetings, and to every place available where someone will listen. It is as if she is saying, "I call out to you men, and young men, listen to my voice. Are you naïve? Then come and learn wisdom. Are you a fool? Then I will give you an understanding heart. Listen to what I say, and you will get excellent advice that is 100 percent accurate. I speak only the truth—anything sinful or wicked is despicable to Me. I speak only righteous words . . .words that are plain to everyone who seeks understanding. I give you accurate information from My vast supply of knowledge. Listen to My instructions and knowledge, and don't chase after silver and gold! My wisdom is worth far more than rubies, silver, or gold—there is nothing of monetary value that begins to compare with what I have to offer."

I, wisdom, live alongside prudence (the ability to govern and discipline oneself). Do you have a deep respect and reverence for the LORD? Then hate evil! Run from pride and arrogance, a wicked lifestyle, and a foul mouth. I, wisdom, own good godly counsel, prudence, and am constantly helping people discover knowledge and how to apply that knowledge daily. Kings and government leaders rule correctly when they use Me; good judicial decisions come from Me. I love those who love Me and who seek Me wholeheartedly. Riches and fame come with Me—yes, riches that endure! The results of finding Me are much better than gold—yes, the finest gold on earth. I lead people in paths of a righteous lifestyle."

The LORD has demonstrated Me (wisdom) since the beginning of creation—long before any of His works were visible. When He made the universe, there I was! When He made the clouds to hold billions and billions of gallons of water and pour it out all over the earth, I was right there! In conclusion, young man, listen to Me and do as I say—then and only then will you be fully blessed by God. Listen carefully, My children, because the person who welcomes and follows My instructions will be richly blessed. There is a special blessing for those who listen carefully to Me, wisdom, anticipating daily what I will say. When you find Me, you will find the essence of life itself and will obtain great favor from the LORD. But, if you turn away from Me, you are sinning against your eternal soul, and the person who hates me is embracing death!

Here is a list of things mentioned in this chapter that embellish God's wisdom:

1. God's wisdom cries out for all people to hear.
2. God's wisdom is aimed especially at the young and naïve.
3. To be a fool, one merely turns away from God's wisdom.
4. God's supply of wisdom and knowledge is inexhaustible.
5. God's wisdom is 100 percent accurate and dependable.
6. It is far better to seek God's wisdom than silver and gold.
7. God's wisdom and the ability to govern one's life go hand in hand.
8. Good judicial decisions come from God's wisdom.
9. To live a righteous life, one must seek God's wisdom.
10. God's wisdom brings a special blessing.

11. To turn away from God's wisdom is to embrace death.

So all of life is based on His eternal and unchanging wisdom. If you want to get ahead and prosper in this life, then embrace His wisdom. He is the epitome of wisdom; He revealed it to us, and when we follow it, our lives here on earth and forever will be far better—so embrace His wisdom!

And how is God's wisdom displayed during a time of judgment? One of the big problems man has is understanding why God, who is so loving and kind, can also bring disaster, calamity, and judgment. Isaiah 31:1–2 addresses this tough question. Israel at that time was getting closer to what we now call "the time of their captivity" when they were taken to Babylon. Some were looking to other nations around them for help, but Isaiah gave them this warning from God. Listen to His words to Israel as He, in His wisdom pleads with them before judgment came: "Woe to those who go down to Egypt for help and rely on horses, who trust in chariots because they are many and in horsemen because they are very strong, but do not look to the Holy One of Israel or consult the LORD! ² And yet he is wise and brings disaster; he does not call back his words, but will arise against the house of the evildoers and against the helpers of those who work iniquity."

He was telling Israel at that point that they were asking for tragedy when they went down to Egypt for help. Do you think their horses, chariots, and many horsemen can help? They look strong, but you should be looking to the Holy One of Israel, seeking help from the LORD. Yet He is *wise* and will bring devastation on your lives. He has given you orders and won't retract His words. He will still punish you for your iniquity and the evil you have done. God, in His infinite wisdom, will come in judgment at exactly the right time—probably just when we think we are secure by leaning on false hope or help from the wrong source. Israel had violated His number one command—don't worship other gods—and now He was coming after them to correct them for their idolatry. In His precise wisdom He knew just when and how to punish them.

How does the wisest man on earth compare to God's infinite wisdom? Jeremiah 10:7 answers that when the prophet speaks of God this way. "Who would not fear you, O King of the nations? For this is your due; for among all the wise ones of the nations and in all their kingdoms there is none like you." The wisest of men doesn't even come close when being compared to our great and wise God!

How is God's wisdom seen in the way He deals with man? One of the great dilemmas in the Old Testament was this: how could the Gentiles ever be included among God's children? In the following verses Paul shows how the wisdom of God embraces all of mankind and how God's wisdom is far superior to man's wisdom. In 1 Corinthians 1:20–25 Paul is contrasting the wisdom of God and the utter foolishness of man. He says, "Where is the one who is wise? Where is the scribe? Where is the debater of this age? Has not God made foolish the wisdom of the world? [21] For since, in the wisdom of God, the world did not know God through wisdom, it pleased God through the folly of what we preach to save those who believe. [22] For Jews demand signs and Greeks seek wisdom, [23] but we preach Christ crucified, a stumbling block to Jews and folly to Gentiles, [24] but to those who are called, both Jews and Greeks, Christ the power of God and the wisdom of God. [25] For the foolishness of God is wiser than men, and the weakness of God is stronger than men."

How will angelic beings see God's wisdom as He deals with man? The Scriptures teach us that, though we can't see them, there are evil angelic beings as well as God's "good angels" (or "holy angels" as they are called twice in Scripture) all around us. Ephesians 3:10 tells us that God intended to show His multifaceted and splendid wisdom through Christ's body, the church, to the various levels of angelic and demonic unseen forces—the principalities and the powers all around us. Psalm 103:20 tells us that angels excel in strength, carrying out each of His commands, and listening intently to every word He speaks. These angelic beings watch the church take shape, and God's wisdom becomes more and more clear to them—and to us!

What glimpses do we have of the wisdom of God in eternity? We read in Revelation 7:9–12, "After this I looked, and behold, a great multitude that no one could number, from every nation, from all tribes and peoples and languages, standing before the throne and before the Lamb, clothed in white robes, with palm branches in their hands, [10] and crying out with a loud voice, "Salvation belongs to our God who sits on the throne, and to the Lamb!" [11] And all the angels were standing around the throne and around the elders and the four living creatures, and they fell on their faces before the throne and worshiped God, [12] saying, "Amen! Blessing and glory and wisdom and thanksgiving and honor and power and might be to our God forever and ever! Amen." We will be able to watch God's wisdom on display for all of eternity! After we are finished with our training course here on earth and are all cleaned up and dressed in white robes—the righteousness of God—then we will be ready to give praise, honor, and glory to Him forever, and rule and reign with Him for all of eternity. What a privilege this will be! Won't it be great to see God's wisdom on display for all of eternity!

Seek

So how do we apply the wisdom of God in our daily lives? When we face any problem or trial in life or just an unpredictable situation, we can look carefully through the Word of God. God has made His wisdom available to us, and as we daily search through the Scriptures, God will reveal to us the exact wisdom we need when we need it to solve the situation we face. This is not just a fantasy; it is reality. God's Spirit reveals to every true believer just the wisdom from God we need. He carefully designed our lives, has a plan for each day of our lives, and will give the necessary wisdom. James 1:5 reminds us that if we need wisdom, we just need to ask of God, who delights in giving to His children what they need. Here are some suggestions in discovering the wisdom of God from the Bible:

1. Look for examples in the Bible of others who applied wisdom and specifically how they applied it to their daily lives.

2. In the Old Testament many good examples of wisdom for daily living are given in the stories. Many of the stories are filled with ways of how to, and how not to do it. For example, when dealing with partiality and favoritism among your children, much is given in the life of Jacob's family on ways not to do it.

3. The book of Proverbs is focused entirely on how to apply the wisdom of God in daily living. Many people have found it helpful to read one chapter of Proverbs each day—the one that corresponds with the day of the month. Solomon covers many topics and in

many cases again tells us how not to do it and what to do to apply God's wisdom to our daily lives.

4. The Law of Moses contains many examples of daily living. For example, dietary laws are never outdated. Many of the "cleansings" and rituals the priests did were practical hygiene steps many doctors and hospitals today have found helpful.

The bottom line is this: God's wisdom is demonstrated to us in many ways throughout the Bible. He shows us how His wisdom is applied in the way He took knowledge and understanding and scientific data and created the universe. Then the Bible beckons us to follow in the pathway of wisdom—that is, taking the principles, laws, commands, examples in people's life stories, etc. and applying them to our daily life. This helps us grasp the wisdom of God He has made available to all men everywhere. Truly He is the God of wisdom!

Man has some wisdom and creative ability and the ability to think through things, but man is also filled with pride and self-sufficiency and self-reliance. *I can do it myself,* we often think. So God puts us in situations where we are forced to see just how helpless we are and how much we need God's strength and wisdom. If we could figure everything out, we wouldn't need God, so He has set circumstances up so that we are forced to turn to Him. Then, when we simply ask Him for the needed wisdom for this situation and this day, He graciously gives it to us. We are in awe as to how much wisdom is available to us. As we get older, we marvel at how much we have learned over the years. If that is true in this life, then how much more will we be able to see throughout eternity the unfolding wisdom of God as He explains to us more and more about His plan for the universe and for us individually? We will always marvel at the vast wisdom of God as it is unfolded to us gradually throughout eternity.

Worship

Pause to Praise and Worship: O God, Your Word tells us that You are the God of wisdom. We see evidences of that wisdom in our world every day. Life seems to us to be like a giant jigsaw puzzle, and as we see each piece fall into place, it all makes more and more sense. Your wisdom is so evident, both in creation and in the way history is falling into place every day—all according to Your marvelous plan. We worship You for the wisdom You used in putting our universe together, and from Your Word we are confident we will see You unfolding Your wisdom to us forever. What a marvelous plan! What a marvelous and great God we serve. Thank You for giving us the wisdom we need every day and for assuring us that the vast supply of wisdom that is Yours will complete the plan for our lives and for all in the universe.

Chapter 11

Incomprehensible: Worth the Effort?

Job 11:7: "Can you find out the deep things of God? Can you find out the limit of the Almighty?"

- How can finite man come to know an infinite God?
- Is God beyond our comprehension?
- How does God come down to earth to meet with man?
- If man were to go looking for God hoping to find Him, where would he go, and where would he start?
- In what ways can man, who is a physical being, have contact with God who is a spirit being?
- What three chapters in the Bible deal with the concept of God's incomprehensibility?

The big challenge: How does one try to explain the incomprehensible God? This is not an attempt to explain God but to see what the Bible says about the fact that God is incomprehensible. This is another of the word descriptions of God that is far beyond man's ability to grasp—that He is incomprehensible. Man tries to figure out something he has made, and with enough effort most can figure out what makes it run or work. But God is in a ballpark all by Himself. Many try to comprehend God by thinking, spiritual meditation, research, asking questions, and they always end up empty-handed. So, if God is beyond our ability to comprehend, why even try? Or is the fact that He reveals Himself as incomprehensible given to us to inspire our worship and praise?

It is as simple as this: Can the thing created ever figure out its Creator? If a man makes a car, or a piece of pottery, or even a garment, can any of these objects even try to comprehend its maker? So if the infinite, awesome God is to be comprehended at any level by man, God chooses how it will be done and how much He will reveal. There is no way the created object—man—can even begin to comprehend his Creator! When God comes to earth to meet with man, how does He do it? Does that help man comprehend God?

Know

God revealed Himself to a few—according to the record—and when He did, He appeared as an angel (referred to many times as the "angel of the Lord," and most hold that these appearances were of the preincarnate Christ); He appeared to Jacob as a man and wrestled with him and to Abraham as a man who sat and ate with him. The first time He appeared to a mass of people was at Mount Sinai; it is described like this in Exodus 20:21: "The people stood far off, and Moses drew near to the thick darkness where God was." In each of these instances, God, who is incomprehensible, chose to reveal Himself to man in a way man could grasp a little more knowledge of who God is. None of these are complete in themselves, but they give man a little more glimpse of the awesomeness, the incomprehensibility of God. One of the tidbits of information about God is that He has the ability to reveal Himself in an infinite number of ways—but that is God!

Let's go back to that scene on Mount Sinai because it speaks so loudly and clearly how our great God, who is unfathomable and incomprehensible, came down and made His presence known to masses of people. This is the time in history when God appeared to a whole nation—Israel—as they were at the base of Mount Sinai. Why did God appear in darkness? God had come down to give to Moses and Israel His unchanging and eternal law, and, because He is a holy God and because of the enormity of the impact of God's law being given to sinful man, God came shrouded in a cloud. Moses told them in verse 20, "Do not fear, for God has come to test you, that the fear of him may be before you, that you may not sin." He was telling them to not be afraid because God came to test you and to cause you to fear Him so they would be restrained from sinning.

Moses recounts this event in Deuteronomy 4:11–12 and said, "And you came near and stood at the foot of the mountain, while the mountain burned with fire to the heart of heaven, wrapped in darkness, cloud, and gloom. ¹² Then the LORD spoke to you out of the midst of the fire. You heard the sound of words, but saw no form; there was only a voice." The only reason Moses went up the mountain and talked face-to-face with God was because God instructed him to do so. In fact, this was such an awesome event when he came face-to-face with the incomprehensible God, and when Moses came down from the mountain, his face shone!

What does the giving of the law on Mount Sinai tell us about man's ability to comprehend an incomprehensible God? Later on, in Deuteronomy 5:22–27, Moses recounted this event again, emphasizing the fire, the cloud, the thick darkness, and "a great voice" that was heard out of the middle of this awesome event. Why the fire, the cloud, the thick darkness, and the loud, booming voice coming out of it? Why didn't God just come out of all of this and sit down and tell the people what was on His heart?

Here are several reasons: first, the Creator is far above and beyond His created beings. He "transcends" them—that is, His position in heaven is so far above what man can comprehend—so much so that God keeps His distance from all created beings. They are near Him, around Him, give praise and glory and honor to Him, but they don't come and sit on His lap and talk to Him. First Timothy 6:16 tells us of God: "…who alone has immortality, who dwells in unapproachable light, whom no one has ever seen or can see. To him be honor and eternal dominion. Amen." These word pictures show us clearly the vast distance between Almighty God and sinful man. The distance between our holy God and sinful man make it impossible for man to comprehend Him. It is not only beyond our ability, but our sinful condition holds us back and makes comprehension even more distant and impossible.

Second, God is holy; that is, He is not evil and cannot be tainted by evil or sin or sinful man. That holiness puts a great distance between

Him and us. Third, the Scriptures record to us that if any sinful man on earth saw the great God of the universe, that man would be instantly consumed—chiefly because man is sinful and God's holiness is pristine and pure and cannot allow sin to be anywhere near His presence. When God came to men on earth—for example, when God and the two angels came to Abraham in Genesis 18—so that Abraham wouldn't be consumed, God veiled Himself in a human body, just as Jesus did when He appeared as a baby. Abraham first thought he was talking with three men, but when the conversation came down to serious spiritual matters and the judgment of God, he knew he was talking with God Himself! (Notice the "He" in verse 10 and the dialogue between the LORD and Abraham in verses 16–32 and verse 33.)

Note how the concept of God's incomprehensibility is shown by Solomon. At the dedication of the man-made temple to the great and holy God when God came down to show His presence and His approval, Solomon said these words in 1 Kings 8:12: "Then Solomon said, 'The LORD has said that he would dwell in thick darkness.'" The thick cloud of darkness veiled or shielded us from His glory, His majesty, and the splendor of His awesome presence, and reminds us of our frailty as we struggle to comprehend our infinite God. Psalm 18:11 reiterates this fact when David says, speaking of the Lord in verses 1 and 6, that He made darkness His secret hiding place. The palace around Him is the darkness of deep ocean waters and the thick clouds, hail, and coals of fire that comes from His presence when He visits anyone here on earth. When God wants to demonstrate to man His greatness and glory, He always comes shrouded in darkness, and His presence brings thick clouds, hail, and bolts of fire. All of this is so hard to comprehend, and that is just the point.

How do we comprehend some of the things God does? Some passages leave our earthly minds in a whirl trying to grasp a little about our God. Psalm 97:2–6 says, "Clouds and thick darkness are all around him; righteousness and justice are the foundation of his throne.³ Fire goes before him and burns up his adversaries all around. ⁴ His lightnings light up the world; the earth sees and trembles. ⁵ The mountains melt like wax before the LORD, before the Lord of all the earth. ⁶ The heavens proclaim his righteousness, and all the peoples see his glory." These awesome descriptions of God's coming to earth tell us of His greatness, His splendor, and His being far beyond man's finite comprehension. Can you imagine "the hills melting like wax at the presence of the LORD, the God of all the earth?"

Does God's incomprehensibility make man look foolish? Eliphaz, the friend of Job from Teman, chided Job by asking him in Job 15:8 if he alone learned the secrets of God? Had he all the wisdom about God to himself? In this statement Eliphaz explained to us that there are many "secrets of God" that man doesn't comprehend. Think of it this way: if man could eventually know "all knowledge, all understanding" and in short know as much as God and comprehend God, what would he need God for after that? He could then just start his own universe, create his own world, and speak all of this into existence! Folly? Yes!

Job's friend from Naamath, Zophar by name, had earlier said in 11:7-10, ""Can you find out the deep things of God? Can you find out the limit of the Almighty? [8] It is higher than heaven—what can you do? Deeper than Sheol—what can you know? [9] Its measure is longer than the earth and broader than the sea. [10] If he passes through and imprisons and summons the court, who can turn him back?"

Just before the LORD spoke to Job out of a violent storm—a whirlwind or a tornado-like storm—Job's fourth friend, Elihu, spoke to Job. Both were trying to understand God and struggled with God's being so far beyond what we can imagine or comprehend.

Job 37:1-13 say this: "At this also my heart trembles and leaps out of its place. [2] Keep listening to the thunder of his voice and the rumbling that comes from his mouth. [3] Under the whole heaven he lets it go, and his lightning to the corners of the earth. [4] After it his voice roars; he thunders with his majestic voice, and he does not restrain the lightnings when his voice is heard. [5] God thunders wondrously with his voice; he does great things that we cannot comprehend. [6] For to the snow he says, 'Fall on the earth,' likewise to the downpour, his mighty downpour. [7] He seals up the hand of every man, that all men whom he made may know it. [8] Then the beasts go into their lairs, and remain in their dens. [9] From its chamber comes the whirlwind, and cold from the scattering winds. [10] By the breath of God ice is given, and the broad waters are frozen fast. [11] He loads the thick cloud with moisture; the clouds scatter his lightning. [12] They turn around and around by his guidance, to accomplish all that he commands them on the face of the habitable world.[13] Whether for correction or for his land or for love, he causes it to happen."

Here is more that points to God's incomprehensibility. Man struggles to find God and understand Him, and Elihu gives us a vast body of information on how God runs His earth! He continued in Job 37: 14-20 saying, "Hear this, O Job; stop and consider the wondrous works of God. [15] Do you know how God lays his command upon them and causes the lightning of his cloud to shine? [16] Do you know the balancings of the clouds, the wondrous works of him who is perfect in knowledge, [17] you whose garments are hot when the earth is still because of the south wind? [18] Can you, like him, spread out the skies, hard as a cast metal mirror? [19] Teach us what we shall say to him; we cannot draw up our case because of darkness. [20] Shall it be told him that I would speak? Did a man ever wish that he would be swallowed up?" Elihu went onto say in verses 21-24, "And now no one looks on the light when it is bright in the skies, when the wind has passed and cleared them. [22] Out of the north comes golden splendor; God is clothed with awesome majesty. [23] The Almighty—we cannot find him; he is great in power; justice and abundant righteousness he will not violate. [24] Therefore men fear him; he does not regard any who are wise in their own conceit." Elihu was saying God is clothed with awesome majesty. When it comes to the Almighty, we can never fully discover all about Him. His power is limitless; His judgment is excellent, accurate, and plentiful. He never afflicts man without a good reason. He does not cater to anyone just because they are smart or wise!

Elihu, in this chapter, tries in many ways to describe our incomprehensible God as He deals with men and as He unveils His mighty power and understanding through what man mistakenly calls "the forces of nature." These are the visible things any person anywhere on earth can witness and with understanding come to the conclusion that God is awesome and man cannot comprehend or begin to comprehend Him!

So where does man begin to get to know just a little bit about such an awesome, incomprehensible God? Solomon in Ecclesiastes 3:11 gave us a hint: "He has made everything beautiful in its time. Also, he has put eternity into man's heart, yet so that he cannot find out what God has done from the beginning to the end." Man's perspective is so small. Man is so confined to this world, space, and time and events that unfold—which man cannot comprehend. Here is the pattern throughout Scripture God uses to demonstrate the huge gap between God and man. First, God tells us what He is about to do through the prophets. Second, then God brings about events with His awesome power; and third, after it is all over, His Spirit reveals to us what just happened. Man has trouble grasping the events of history and putting them together coherently; so God helps fill in the gaps and in doing so demonstrates to man that he can't really comprehend what He is doing.

To demonstrate in another way how incomprehensible God is, look at the life of Jesus. No one during Jesus's lifetime knew what was happening and understood the events of His life until after it was all over and He had ascended back into heaven. Then, through the words He spoke and looking back at what the prophets said in telling of His coming and the purpose for it, the Spirit of God unveiled to the apostles what had just happened. God spoke so clearly that today we can look back and explain in great detail who Jesus Christ was, why He came, what He accomplished, and then get somewhat of an idea what is about to happen as He returns to finish that work!

When we look backward in time at how God judged the world and cleaned up the mess that it was in at that time, then we will have great understanding about the tribulation, the rapture, the way God chose to deal with the nations and His special people Israel, and why Armageddon, the judgment seat of Christ, the lake of fire, and the great white throne judgment are necessary. *Right now* we see through a glass, and see things very dimly; but then we will have much greater understanding as we see God face-to-face (see 1 Corinthians 13:12). This seems frustrating to us now, but that is an example of how we will for eternity be dealing with a feeble attempt to comprehend God.

These are just a few of the steps God has taken to unveil His plan to man. In the unveiling of that plan, we understand much more about Him, but there is still much we don't understand because man is not able to comprehend God. He, His plan, and His character must be seen one step at a time, one more unfolding of events that shape history—so much so that man will never complete the job of trying to comprehend and discover the height and breadth and depth of God. Isaiah 55:8–9 sums it up in these words: "For my thoughts are not your thoughts, neither are your ways my ways, declares the LORD. ⁹ For as the heavens are higher than the earth, so are my ways higher than your ways and my thoughts than your thoughts. So when we get a glimpse of God, we do seem very small!"

Seek

One of the great challenges in trying to fathom God is to look at ourselves in the light of what He can do. Here are some haunting questions and strong statements about God's incomprehensibility: Isaiah 40:12–31 says, "Who has measured the waters in the hollow of his hand and marked off the heavens with a span, enclosed the dust of the earth in a measure and weighed the mountains in scales and the hills in a balance? ¹³ Who has measured the Spirit of the LORD, or what man shows him his counsel? ¹⁴ Whom did he consult, and who made him understand? Who taught him the path of justice, and taught him knowledge, and showed him the way of understanding? ¹⁵ Behold, the nations are like a drop from a bucket, and are accounted as the dust on the scales; behold, he takes up the coastlands like fine dust. ¹⁶ Lebanon would not suffice for fuel, nor are its beasts enough for a burnt offering. ¹⁷ All the nations are as nothing before him, they are accounted by him as less than nothing and emptiness. ¹⁸ To whom then will you liken God, or what likeness compare with him? ¹⁹ An idol! A craftsman casts it, and a goldsmith overlays it with gold and casts for it silver chains. ²⁰ He who is too impoverished for an offering chooses wood that will not rot; he seeks out a skillful craftsman to set up an idol that will not move. ²¹ Do you not know? Do you not hear? Has it not been told you from the beginning? Have you not understood from the foundations of the earth? ²² It is he who sits above the circle of the earth, and its inhabitants are like grasshoppers; who stretches out the heavens like a curtain, and spreads them like a tent to dwell in; ²³ who brings princes to nothing, and makes the rulers of the earth as emptiness. ²⁴ Scarcely are they planted, scarcely sown, scarcely has their stem taken root in the earth, when he blows on them, and they wither, and the tempest carries them off like stubble. [25] To whom then will you compare me, that I should be like him? says the Holy One. [26] Lift up your eyes on high and see: who created these? He who brings out their host by number, calling them all by name; by the greatness of his might and because he is strong in power, not one is missing. [27] Why do you say, O Jacob, and speak, O Israel, 'My way is hidden from the LORD, and my right is disregarded by my God'? [28] Have you not known? Have you not heard? The LORD is the everlasting God, the Creator of the ends of the earth. He does not faint or grow weary; his understanding is unsearchable. [29] He gives power to the faint, and to him who has no might he increases strength. [30] Even youths shall faint and be weary, and young men shall fall exhausted; [31] but they who wait for the LORD shall renew their strength; they shall mount up with wings like eagles; they shall run and not be weary; they shall walk and not faint."

Isaiah in this passage was pointing out the greatness and infinite character of God and that He is totally incomprehensible. Words fall far short to describe God, but we have been left with many word pictures that convey to us more about God. We try to fathom Him, and today we use scientific knowledge to search out more about what He made in six creation days. He created this world and the universe in six days, and man has been trying for six thousand years to figure out what He did and how He did it. But since God is incomprehensible, the best we can do is accept what He said happened and how it happened and then fall at His feet in worship and praise. Isn't that what the great and awesome God has been trying to get us to do all of this time?

As a believer seeks God, there is so much that we have overlooked in the Holy Scriptures that could help us if we would but take the time and effort to search. Again, we can return to Solomon's words in Proverbs 1; he was the wisest man on earth, past, present, and future, and he instructed us to "search for the treasures of wisdom in the Scriptures with the zeal we would use to find a gold mine." God will reveal to us much more than we can imagine, but the effort by a believer to do the searching and allow the Holy Spirit to guide him is the one missing ingredient. We must provide that!

Worship

Pause to Praise and Worship: O God, You made clear that finite man will never fully comprehend You, the infinite God, but at the same time You put in our hearts a capacity to worship and then gave us the tools with which we could find out much about You. Help us not to be discouraged by the fact that it is overwhelming the amount that we have yet to discover about You; instead, help us use this as a way to bow in worship and praise to You. You desire us to have a worshipping heart toward You and You alone, so we ask You to light a fire of intensity about our lives that causes us to search and find You when we search for You with all our hearts. To that end we dedicate the rest of our existence, and at each step along the way, we will pause to worship and praise You—even though we will never fully comprehend You. We praise You! We honor You!

Chapter 12

Holy: God Is Holy, but Me Holy?

Psalm 99:5, "Exalt the LORD our God; worship at his footstool! Holy is he!"

- That does it mean to be holy, or what is holiness?
- Is God the only One who is holy?
- Has He always been holy?
- Do you know anyone who is holy?
- Is anyone on earth holy?
- Is holiness beyond the grasp of sinful man?
- Can holiness be attained in this lifetime?
- Who, in the Bible, referred to God as holy?

Many of the character qualities or attributes of God are hard for finite man to grasp, but this one is the hardest! As pointed out before, God is all powerful, but man has a little power; God is present everywhere, but man is present only in one place at a time; God is good, but man can at times be good; God has infinite knowledge, but man has at least a little bit of knowledge; etc. But one character quality God alone possesses, and man is totally devoid of, is holiness! Romans 3:10–11 quotes from at least three Old Testament references and reaffirms that not one person on earth is righteous—no, not even one! No one understands his lost condition and seeks God. Yet the Bible says over and over that God is holy and righteous. No sin has or can contaminate Him and His holy presence.

Know

The Bible says that God is holy—that is He is good, righteous, and not tainted by sin; nor can He be tainted by any sin. He is spotless and has no bad streak or bad quality about Him; not only that but God has never done wrong, nor can He do wrong. To be holy means to be set apart from sin and evil and unable even to be contaminated with sin.

Holiness is so hard to grasp because the only holiness a man can have is a gift given through Jesus Christ as He comes into a person's life, cleans him up, and makes him holy. The best way to grasp what it means that God is holy is to have the Scriptures define it and describe it to us.

What reaction should man have to the holiness of God? When Moses came near the burning bush in Exodus 3:5, God said to him, "...Do not come near; take your sandals off your feet, for the place on which you are standing is holy ground." God was saying, "Don't come any closer! Take your shoes off because you are standing on holy ground." Wherever God is, that place is holy; and so as Moses, out of curiosity, approached the bush that was burning yet was not consumed, he didn't know that he was approaching a meeting with his Holy God, so he was instructed to remove his shoes. Ordinary dirt was turned into holy ground because God was near. This scene was again repeated to Joshua, Moses's successor, in Joshua 5:15: "And the commander of the LORD's army said to Joshua, 'Take off your sandals from your feet, for the place where you are standing is holy.' And Joshua did so." The *"Commander-in-chief"* of heaven's armies told Joshua to take off his shoes because he was standing on holy ground. So Joshua obeyed, and we would have done the same thing.

Compared to other gods, how does our God stack up? Is He really holy? Exodus 15:11 says, "Who is like you, O LORD, among the gods? Who is like you, majestic in holiness, awesome in glorious deeds, doing wonders?"

Throughout the book of Leviticus are many references to God's holy character. When God instituted the Levitical priesthood, He gave these specific instructions in Leviticus 21:6–8, and He told Moses to pass on these instructions to the Levites: Aaron's sons would be set apart in a special way for their God. That way they wouldn't contaminate God's holy name and reputation. Their job was to offer the holy bread of God and the fire offerings and sacrifices to God. For that reason they must be specifically and specially set apart from all other people. Also, for that reason, they could not marry a sexually immoral woman. Why? Because that priest is holy and set apart for God alone. So you, Moses, must set him apart for a holy life because his life is totally dedicated to offering the holy bread to God. That's why each priest must be set apart from his people. I am the Lord; I am holy, and I set each of you apart for a clean, pure life.

When we see these instructions that seem so foreign to us, we begin to understand a little about God's holy character as He set apart the priests for Himself. The bottom line is this: the various instructions for the priests, the cleansings they went through, and all of the ceremonies they went through demonstrated His holiness to Israel. The idea of holiness is throughout these instructions. They were told to be "set apart" for God. God's holy character demands that the priest must be separated from others and live life on a higher standard. This is a picture how God is separated from us sinful human beings because of His holiness and our sin.

What makes any place on earth holy? Answer: the presence of God. The one place God chose to dwell on earth for a period of time in Israel's glory days was the temple. Many times this temple was referred to as "God's holy temple." Psalm 11:4 says, "The Lord is in His holy temple, the Lord's throne is in heaven: His eyes behold, His eyelids try, the children of men." Here we are told that the Lord continually resides in His holy temple. His throne is in heaven, and His eyes are constantly watching and evaluating each person on earth. It is unnerving to us to imagine a great God who is constantly watching everything that we do and say! But then, God is holy and we are sinful, so He must keep an eye on us! Exodus 15:13 adds this: "You have led in your steadfast love the people whom you have redeemed; you have guided them by your strength to your holy abode." God's temple was holy because God was there, and Israel is a holy place because the God of the entire universe lived there, and since He is holy every place He goes becomes holy when He arrives!

Why is Jerusalem referred to as "the Holy City," and what makes that city holy? Psalm 48:1, in speaking of Mount Zion, or Jerusalem, says,

"Great is the LORD and greatly to be praised in the city of our God! His holy mountain." Almighty God chose to place His name and reputation in the city of Jerusalem. When God dwells in His Mount Zion, His presence there makes it a "holy place."

Where does holiness reign supreme? Psalm 47:8 points out this fact: "God reigns over the nations; God sits on his holy throne." What would happen if God were not holy, just, and righteous? And if He allowed those who had not become righteous by Jesus's blood to be part of His kingdom? Even the smallest taint of sin or unrighteousness, and we would be destroying one another. But His holiness ensures us that we are and will have that "love for one another," which we are exhorted to develop while here on earth, and that love will keep all of the believers of all time, loving one another for all of eternity. Love is the "superglue" that holds the body of Christ together because we have become holy as He is holy!

Who set the standard of holiness? Does His holiness make Him distinct from man? Isaiah 5:16 is a powerful verse on our great holy God. "But the LORD of hosts is exalted in justice, and the Holy God shows himself holy in righteousness." Here we find that the Lord, the Commander in chief of this universe, will be shown to be thorough and accurate in all His decisions as Judge. He is the holy God, and His righteous standards and His character set Him apart. The more we look at how the Bible describes our God as being great and holy, the smaller and smaller we feel in His sight. His holiness sets Him apart distinctively from man. The fact that a judge must be holy to be 100 percent accurate shows us why man makes a poor judge.

Does God's holiness distinguish Him greatly from mortal man? Psalm 60:6 and 108:7 tell us that God has spoken in His holiness, and I will rejoice about that. In Psalm 89:35, when God made an absolute promise to King David that his descendants would sit on the throne forever, He said, "Once for all I have sworn by my holiness; I will not lie to David." He said it once, and His holiness backs up what He said, and He would not lie to David. These verses point out to us that whenever God speaks, we can rest assured that He *always* speaks in holiness—everything He says flows from that one character quality (which is important for sinful man to remember).

How can man respect and reverence God as holy? One way is by the words that come out of our mouths. Many people today "use God's name in vain"; that is, they swear and cuss. Psalm 111:9 speaks to this evil by saying, "He sent redemption to his people; he has commanded his covenant forever. Holy and awesome is his name!" This tells us that God sent redemption to His people. He has permanently assured us that His covenant promises will be forever—and to seal it He reminds us that His name is holy and to be held in highest esteem. Little in our day is "sacred" or "holy," but the name of God is holy, and we must hold His name with the deepest reverence.

How does God's holiness inspire men to worship Him? And a related question: why is King David such an inspiration to believers? One of the reasons King David has been held up by Almighty God as a great role model for the rest of us is this: who else has inspired more people to worship and praise God with his writings than King David? In Psalm 95:1–5, 9, the psalmist exalts God's name like this: "The LORD reigns; let the peoples tremble! He sits enthroned upon the cherubim; let the earth quake! ² The LORD is great in Zion; he is exalted over all the peoples. ³ Let them praise your great and awesome name! Holy is he! ⁴ The King in his might loves justice. You have established equity; you have executed justice and righteousness in Jacob. ⁵ Exalt the LORD our God; worship at his footstool! Holy is he! . . . Exalt the LORD our God, and worship at his holy mountain; for the LORD our God is holy!" How many times must we be reminded that the LORD, our God, is holy? Psalm 105:3 chimes in by saying, "Glory in his holy name; let the hearts of those who seek the LORD rejoice!"

Will God and His holy name ever be held in high regard on earth? Ezekiel 39:25 says, "Therefore thus says the Lord GOD: Now I will restore the fortunes of Jacob and have mercy on the whole house of Israel, and I will be jealous for my holy name." Ezekiel 36:21–23 continues the thought: "But I had concern for my holy name, which the house of Israel had profaned among the nations to which they came. ²² Therefore say to the house of Israel, Thus says the Lord GOD: It is not for your sake, O house of Israel, that I am about to act, but for the sake of my holy name, which you have profaned among the nations to which you came. ²³ And I will vindicate the holiness of my great name, which has been profaned among the nations, and which you have profaned among them. And the nations will know that I am the LORD, declares the Lord GOD, when through you I vindicate my holiness before their eyes." We too, as Christians in the era, have this responsibility to keep the name of God as holy before a world that is watching us carefully. When we are exalting His holy name, we are telling a watching world how great our God is.

Does this world ever get a glimpse of God's holiness? Isaiah 52:10 tells us that to redeem Israel, "The LORD has bared his holy arm before the eyes of all the nations, and all the ends of the earth shall see the salvation of our God." When God decides to demonstrate His awesome power, it is overwhelming force, and all the nations watch in awe—like when He brought Israel out of Egypt. And at that point they too saw His holiness on display.

Another major question is this: Is God really the only One who is holy? The Bible tells us "yes!" Holiness is the foundation of His throne. He sets the standard as to what is good and holy and righteous, and if any other creature is pronounced "holy," it is because they have mirrored His pristine holiness.

In the following verses note how God is described as being holy, and the descriptions vary greatly.

- God is the only One who is holy. First Samuel 2:2: "There is none holy like the LORD: for there is none besides you; there is no rock like our God." This verse also points out once again that the standard for each character quality man is to emulate is set by God Himself. Holiness is a character quality possessed only by Him—and those who by faith become His "holy children." Job 4:17 reaffirms this, saying, "Can mortal man be in the right before God? Can a man be pure before his Maker?"
- God Himself says that He is holy. The verses previously listed all say at least once that "God is holy" or "I am holy." Other references are: Leviticus 11:44–45; 19:2; and 20:26.
- The four creatures who are constantly around the throne proclaiming God's holiness keep emphasizing it again and

again. This is the sole purpose of their existence. Isaiah 6:3 and Revelation 4:8 say, "And the four living creatures, each of them with six wings, are full of eyes all around and within, and day and night they never cease to say, 'Holy, holy, holy, is the Lord God Almighty, who was and is and is to come!'"

- God is referred to by those in Israel as "the Holy One of Israel." Isaiah 12:6 says, "Shout, and sing for joy, O inhabitant of Zion, for great in your midst is the Holy One of Israel." Isaiah 29:19 refers to God as the Holy One of Israel: "The meek shall obtain fresh joy in the LORD, and the poor among mankind shall exult in the Holy One of Israel." Isaiah 29:23 adds that when Jacob sees His children all around him—the ones God made with His hands, then they will reverence and respect God's name and call Him "the Holy One of Jacob," and, in doing so, show respect and reverence for the God of Israel. The Jews remind us again and again to show great respect and reverence for God and for God's holy name. (Other references are Isaiah 41:14, 16, 20; 43:2–3, 14–15; 47:4; 49:7; and Ezekiel 39:7.)

Seek

How are believers to become holy? The thing that strikes sinful man is when God calls believers His holy children (or saints). Over and over in the Bible He tells us, His followers, "Be holy, because I am holy!" How can a sinful man become holy? The Scriptures explain to us that *when* the sacrifice of Jesus' death and His blood is applied to our lives and to our sins, they are gone—forever! When we, by God's grace, receive God's gift of salvation, we are cleaned up—so much so that now God refers to those who are born again as "saints" or "His holy children."

Leviticus 11:44–45 says, "For I am the LORD your God. Consecrate yourselves therefore, and be holy, for I am holy. You shall not defile yourselves with any swarming thing that crawls on the ground. 45 For I am the LORD who brought you up out of the land of Egypt to be your God. You shall therefore be holy, for I am holy." A believer can do much to move away from evil and toward God's holiness, as we must become holy.

God repeats the same thing to them in Leviticus 19:2 and 20:26. In that last verse God told the Israelites that they were to be holy because He is holy because He had severed them from other peoples so they should be totally His. This reinforces the idea that one of the ways to describe being holy is to be separate from the world around us—literally to be severed from them. That is the only way we can "be holy as God is holy."

Believers must come often to the "fountain filled with blood" and confess our sins, and each time He will forgive! First John 1:9 says, "If we confess our sins, he is faithful and just to forgive us our sins and to cleanse us from all unrighteousness." Then, once again we are holy because we are cleansed from sin and forgiven each time we confess.

In 1 Peter 1:15–16, Peter says, "…but as he who called you is holy, you also be holy in all your conduct, [16] since it is written, 'You shall be holy, for I am holy.'" Just as God who called you and put His hand on your life is holy, so you must also be holy throughout all of your life. Why? Because God's eternal Word says, 'You are to be holy because I am holy.'" *Imagine this:* we have the privilege of being one of God's holy children—and He calls us "holy"! His holiness must permeate every part of our lives.

What is a practical way man can put aside his sin and embrace God's holiness? Listen to this exchange between Joshua about the time of his death and the nation of Israel in Joshua 24:16–24: "Then the people answered, "Far be it from us that we should forsake the Lord to serve other gods, [17] for it is the LORD our God who brought us and our fathers up from the land of Egypt, out of the house of slavery, and who did those great signs in our sight and preserved us in all the way that we went, and among all the peoples through whom we passed. [18] And the LORD drove out before us all the peoples, the Amorites who lived in the land. Therefore we also will serve the LORD, for he is our God. [19] But Joshua said to the people, 'You are not able to serve the LORD, for he is a holy God. He is a jealous God; he will not forgive your transgressions or your sins. [20] If you forsake the LORD and serve foreign gods, then he will turn and do you harm and consume you, after having done you good.' [21] And the people said to Joshua, "No, but we will serve the LORD." [22] Then Joshua said to the people, 'You are witnesses against yourselves that you have chosen the LORD, to serve him." And they said, 'We are witnesses.' [23] He said, 'Then put away the foreign gods that are among you, and incline your heart to the LORD, the God of Israel.' ^{24} And the people said to Joshua, "The LORD our God we will serve, and his voice we will obey.'"

Did Israel always obey God throughout their history? Joshua pointed out in this passage that one way man can become holy is to totally turn away from idolatry, and Israel dabbled with idolatry throughout all of their history and were eventually sent into captivity because of their idolatry. Every generation must turn away from idols and idolatry and worship God.

The Ark of the Covenant in Israel was the place where their holy God resided among them. What happened when some Israelites defied God's order and looked—even at a symbol of God's holiness?

The only time recorded in Scripture that the Ark of the Covenant was taken from Israel was during the time when Samuel judged Israel, and it was just after a battle with the Philistines. When the heathen people of Philistia had enough of the plagues that came when they had the ark, they sent it back to Israel. The ark ended up in a city called Beth Shemesh, and scores of people had the ark uncovered and looked at it. This was forbidden since the day the ark was made. Only the high priest could come into the "holiest of holy" places with a blood sacrifice for the people's sins for that year, and then only once a year, and this happened on the Day of Atonement.

When these people of Beth Shemesh looked at the ark, 50,070 of them were killed for gawking at the ark—doing what had been forbidden. In disbelief and shock, the people of that city said, "Can anyone stand before this holy God? Who will take it from us back to Shiloh?" This emphasizes strongly to us the holiness of our God and how serious it is to break His commands to us, especially when it comes to the sacred objects He has made holy. In this instance His holiness had been offended and was thoroughly judged.

How did Job exalt his Holy God? In the midst of his tragic life, he was determined not to accuse or blame God but instead to emphasize God's holy character. Job, crying out in the anguish of his heart, says in Job 6:8–10, "Oh that I might have my request, and that God would fulfill my hope, ^{9} that it would please God to crush me, that he would let loose his hand and cut me off! ^{10} This would be my comfort; I would even exult in pain unsparing, for I have not denied the words of the Holy One." He knew that God, being holy, would have revealed his sin to him (if he had sinned), yet he chose to speak highly of God's holy character even in the midst of his tragic life.

Later in Job 34:10, Job's fourth friend, Elihu, says to Job's three other "friends," "Therefore, hear me, you men of understanding: far be it from God that he should do wickedness, and from the Almighty that he should do wrong."

Job's life is a fascinating contrast between what our adversary, Satan, wants to do to us and what Job was convinced his holy God was doing. Here's the begging question: at what point did he realize what had happened in chapters 1 and 2? Here's the secret: he knew that God is holy and doesn't do anything evil, so it must have been his adversary, the devil, who got permission from Almighty God to launch his attack against Job. (Note in the margin of many Bibles that the name of Satan in Job chapters 1 and 2 is the word "adversary.") I also believe that when Job heard God speak to him out of the whirlwind (in chapters 38-41), he knew for sure that it wasn't God that had launched the attack against him in chapters 1 and 2!

Can our Holy God have any evil blamed on Him? Elihu says again in Job 36:23 and speaking of God, "Who has prescribed for him his way, or who can say, 'You have done wrong'?" He was asking, "Who has told God how He should live? Or who can say to God, 'You have done wrong to me.'" The point is this: no man can attribute evil or wrongdoing to God because He is holy.

Why is God alone holy? Why can that holiness never change? Listen to what Hosea 11:9 says quoting God, "I will not execute my burning anger; I will not again destroy Ephraim; for I am God and not a man, the Holy One in your midst, and I will not come in wrath." So God can never be anything but holy because it is part of His character, and He cannot ever change! Thanks be to God forever for that!

How does the fact that God allowed the heathen to exist bring out God's holiness? Habakkuk 1:12 is a powerful verse that accents God's holy character: "Are you not from everlasting, O LORD my God, my Holy One? We shall not die. O LORD, you have ordained them as a judgment, and you, O Rock, have established them for reproof." He was asking,

"Have You not always existed, O LORD my God, my Holy God?" In contrast, we will only live from this moment on! You, O Lord, have created and destined the heathen for judgment. And O mighty God, You allowed them to exist so that You could correct them! This verse points out the fact that because God is holy, His holiness demands that the heathen be punished forever. Isn't that a statement as to why God allowed the heathen to exist and why sin is in our world? That fact makes God's holiness that much more pristine and pronounced.

What is man's response to God's holiness as it is unveiled in the Bible? The answer is in Isaiah 57:15: "For thus says the One who is high and lifted up, who inhabits eternity, whose name is Holy: 'I dwell in the high and holy place, and also with him who is of a contrite and lowly spirit, to revive the spirit of the lowly, and to revive the heart of the contrite.'" Here is a message to everyone from the Supreme Ruler of the universe, the One who lives in the "eternal now," and the One whose name is Holy: "I live in the number one spot in all of the universe, on My throne in heaven; *but* I also live in the heart of every person who has a broken and a crushed heart before Me and has a humble heart! My purpose is to bring back to life those who humble themselves and revive the heart of everyone whose heart is broken and crushed before Me." Isaiah pointed out not only what God desires to do in the heart of a sinful man but also what His holiness can do for man. His holiness is involved in raising up and bringing back to life every person whose heart is humble and broken before Him.

How can I begin to appreciate God's holiness? Many people want to know how to understand and know God. Proverbs 9:10 tells us how to do that. "The fear of the LORD is the beginning of wisdom, and the knowledge of the Holy One is insight." Here we find that the starting place of acquiring wisdom is found in developing a deep respect, reverence, and fear of God. Also, understanding begins to come to a person when he gets to know God as being holy. So the "fear of God," the one ingredient that is essential and which fosters respect and reverence for God, is the starting place for wisdom to develop, and knowing God as holy begins the process in developing understanding.

Does God's holiness ignite our heart in praise and worship? First Chronicles 16:10–11 exhorts us to "Glory in his holy name; let the hearts of those who seek the LORD rejoice! [11] Seek the LORD and his strength; seek his presence continually!" Nothing in this world ignites praise, honor, glory, and thanks from the heart of man like the pristine character of our great God! When we gather together, we remind ourselves of His many awe-inspiring character qualities, and we burst forth in praise to Him. This is merely a tune-up for our eternal occupation when we will gather many times to worship our magnificent God. Psalm 22:3 furthers the thought: "Yet you are holy, enthroned on the praises of Israel." The psalmist is saying, "God, You are holy, and Your righteousness, purity, and holiness are the focus of the praise of all of Your children." Psalm 30:4 tells us, "Sing praises to the LORD, O you his saints, and give thanks to his holy name." David was saying, "Burst forth with singing to the LORD, all you His holy children, and give thanks whenever you think about His holiness."

In the concluding book of the Bible, Revelation, when Jesus Christ will be unveiled to this world in judgment, we find a good many scenes where John describes those who have gathered to worship God. The first scenes are in chapters 4 and 5, and right in the middle of those scenes we are introduced to the "seraphim," or living creatures, and they are the ones whose eternal occupation is to announce and accentuate the holiness of our God. The scene unveiled to us is one where all believers of all time will gather to worship God, and one of the things we will worship Him for is for His holiness. This one character quality of God is displayed to us as one of those that will ignite our worship of God forever. Revelation 15:4 says, "Who will not fear, O Lord, and glorify your name? For you alone are holy. All nations will come and worship you, for your righteous acts have been revealed." The song of Moses asks us if anyone can fail to show respect, reverence, and fear God?

- Who can fail to be involved in bringing glory and honor to His name?
- Because He alone is God, and He is holy.
- All the nations will come and bow down in worship before Him.
- Why? Because His judicial decisions are well known everywhere.
- Even the angels who haven't been tarnished by sin will join us in praise to God for His holy character. The angels who haven't sinned will see God's holiness from the perspective of having never

sinned, and we will join them because we too have been cleansed from all of our sin and understand His holiness from a totally different perspective.

- Together we and all other creatures in God's great heaven will express forever our praise and honor and wisdom and worship for God's holiness. What a privilege that will be!

Worship

Pause to Praise and Worship: O God, what a privilege to bow before You, both now and throughout eternity, because You are holy. We can't fathom Your holiness (and little else about Your character), but we bow gladly and with hearts bursting with praise and thanksgiving. How can You take a wicked, vile sinner like me and make me holy through the blood of Jesus Christ? We praise You because You have done this, and this too will ignite our hearts forever in worship and praise. You alone are holy!

Conclusion

Romans 11:33–36: "Oh, the depth of the riches and wisdom and knowledge of God! How unsearchable are his judgments and how inscrutable his ways! ³⁴ 'For who has known the mind of the Lord, or who has been his counselor?' ³⁵ 'Or who has given a gift to him that he might be repaid?' ³⁶ For from him and through him and to him are all things. To him be glory forever. Amen."

How does one close a brief book whose main aim is to point others to the character of our great God and how redeemed man is destined to showcase forever God's *holiness, mercy, love,* and *forgiveness*? We are carefully taught in the Bible how to come to know God—both initially in salvation and then through His Word as we study it; then we are aware that we are urged to seek the Lord with all our hearts; and that when we seek Him, we will find Him when we search for Him with all of our hearts. (Jeremiah 29:13). Finally, we discover that the purpose of these instructions is to prepare us to worship and praise Him forever. So, to summarize the main focus of this book, let's take a look at what the Scriptures tell us about the "temple" of God.

The first time the temple is referred to in Scripture is when Moses was shown a "pattern" for building the tabernacle in the wilderness. Moses was given a glimpse of the temple of God in heaven through a supernatural revelation, and he was instructed in Exodus 25 and Numbers 8 to be careful to make the tabernacle in the wilderness according to the pattern he had been shown when he was up on the mountain.

Heaven is a huge expanse of space and real estate, but the center place in all of heaven (and in the universe) is the temple of God—the place where God resides—the central command post of the universe, and in that temple all believers of all time will eventually be completely united and come often to worship God.

But the tabernacle in the wilderness, and later Solomon's temple, was a place where men on earth would gather to worship God. The Gentiles were not allowed in or to participate in the actual activities of offering sacrifices, but they were beckoned to come to worship God. Solomon's temple was by far the greatest and most magnificent one built on earth, and it is far beyond our comprehension! Everything seems to have been overlaid with gold, and all nations of the earth came there to worship God.

But that is Old Testament stuff, right? When Jesus Christ came and fulfilled all of the Mosaic Law and the prophets, all of that passed away forever, right? No! Let's take a look at the other temples mentioned in the Scripture.

1. The first place(s) of worship mentioned in the Bible were the altars that were built by Abel, Abraham, Isaac, Jacob, etc., and these Old Testament saints worshipped their great God there.

2. The first structure built for a centralized meeting place was the tabernacle in the wilderness. It was made of animal skins for curtains to shield man from the glory of God revealed in it, and Israel came here to bring their sacrifices and worship God.

3. Next was Solomon's temple—the first permanent structure built on earth, and all nations of the earth—that is, those who were believers—came there to worship (for example, the queen of Sheba along with all of her court).

4. The next temple built was in the days of Ezra and Nehemiah. This temple was a bit smaller, and its glory was not as great as Solomon's temple, but it was again a place for God's people to gather and worship Him.

5. The next one mentioned was Herod's temple. The most significant thing about this temple was that Jesus came there to be dedicated to God, and He worshipped God there while He was on earth.

6. Today we are waiting for the next temple to be built—this one is referred to by evangelicals as "the tribulation temple." In this one the Antichrist will come and mock God and proclaim himself to

be "god." This one is referred to many times in Scripture, but its historical significance is that it is the one built just before "the day of the Lord," the day when Jesus Christ comes to wipe out "the nations of the world who have gathered together to finally wipe out Israel."

7. Next we come to the last earthly temple—the one mentioned by Ezekiel in chapters 40–48. But why this temple? I thought Jesus came and fulfilled all of the Mosaic sacrificial laws and that now we enter boldly into the presence of God at any place on earth that we happen to be; isn't all we have to do is to pause and bow our hearts in worship and praise to Him anytime, anywhere? When this temple is built, *all believers worldwide* are instructed to come and worship God—and if you don't, it won't rain on your land when you get home (Zechariah 14:17–18)!

Here is the main point of each of these temples: each is only a small glimpse of the magnificent temple of God that is in heaven. John saw this temple in his visions in the book of Revelation, and in each of these times, he saw worship of God taking place where redeemed men, angels, and other living creatures gather often to worship God.

To whet our appetite for heaven, let's look into one of these throne scenes in Revelation 5. Here we are introduced to the Lamb of God in all of His glory and splendor, when all believers of all time gather in this magnificent temple to worship God and to watch the coronation of Jesus Christ our Lord. What is fascinating about this scene is that when this "scroll" was opened and the seals broken, and when the prayers of God's holy children are fully answered, "a new song is sung," and here are the words to that new song in Revelation 5:9-10: "And they sang a new song, saying, 'Worthy are you to take the scroll and to open its seals, for you were slain, and by your blood you ransomed people for God from every tribe and language and people and nation, [10] and you have made them a kingdom and priests to our God, and they shall reign on the earth.'"

At this point John saw angels coming from every direction of the universe! They were saying, "You aren't going to have a 'Praise to the Lamb celebration' without us!" And they then joined with their voices—and the number of them was hundreds of millions—and all of them saying with a loud voice, "Worthy is the Lamb who was slain, to receive power and wealth and wisdom and might and honor and glory and blessing!" [13] And I heard every creature in heaven and on earth and under the earth and in the sea, and all that is in them, saying, 'To him who sits on the throne and to the Lamb be blessing and honor and glory and might forever and ever!" [14] And the four living creatures said, "Amen!" and the elders fell down and worshiped." What a praise gathering this is going to be, and this is just a prelude of what we will do throughout all of eternity—praising God because of His awesome character. We will then have the privilege of joining these praise gatherings in the temple of God and around His throne! Wow! I can hardly wait!

We began this book by asking why we need to study God. If we don't know who God is and understand what the Bible tells us about Him, then how will we be ready to spend eternity worshipping and praising Him? And in the careful studying of God we find many of man's basic questions answered. This is important because when our questions are answered and we go on to discover more and more about our God, then it is clear from the Bible that our hearts will be ignited in praise and worship—forever. Each character quality unveils to us a little more about God, and God has put it in word pictures. This helps us see as much as we are able in this life so that we can begin our "forever occupation"—worshipping and praising God—and we can start now. When we worship and praise God, then we begin to fulfill our purpose for existence. Worship and praise of God is the most important thing we can do any day of our lives. The psalmist in Psalm 119:164 said, "Seven times a day I praise you for your righteous rules." Let's begin now to praise and worship our God, worship Him often, learn much from His Word about how to worship Him, and then be ready for eternity. It is coming soon!

Afterword

Psalm 145
(A final burst of praise: a psalm of King David)
(Italicized are references to God's character.)

¹ I will extol you, my God and *King*, and bless your name *forever and ever*.

² Every day I will bless you and praise your name *forever and ever*.

³ *Great* is the LORD, and greatly to be praised, and his *greatness* is *unsearchable*.

⁴ One generation shall commend your works to another, and shall declare your mighty acts.

⁵ On the *glorious splendor of your majesty*, and on your *wondrous works*, I will meditate.

⁶ They shall speak of the *might of your awesome deeds*, and I will declare your *greatness*.

⁷ They shall pour forth the fame of your abundant *goodness* and shall sing aloud of your *righteousness*.

⁸ The LORD is *gracious* and *merciful, slow to anger* and abounding in steadfast love.

⁹ The LORD is *good* to all, and his *mercy* is over all that *he has made*.

¹⁰ *All your works* shall give thanks to you, O LORD, and all your saints shall bless you!

¹¹ They shall speak of the *glory* of your kingdom and tell of your *power*,

¹² to make known to the children of man your *mighty deeds*, and the *glorious splendor* of your kingdom.

¹³ Your kingdom is an *everlasting* kingdom, and your dominion *endures throughout all generations*. [The LORD is *faithful* in all his words and *kind* in all his works.]

¹⁴ The LORD *upholds* all who are falling and raises up all who are bowed down.

[15] The eyes of all *look* to you, and you *give them their food* in due season.

[16] *You open* your hand; you *satisfy the desire* of every living thing.

[17] The LORD is *righteous* in all his ways and *kind* in all his works.

[18] The LORD *is near* to all who call on him, to all *who call* on him in truth.

[19] He *fulfills the desire* of those who fear him; he also *hears their cry* and *saves* them.

[20] The LORD *preserves* all who love him, but all the *wicked he will destroy.*

[21] My mouth will speak the *praise* of the LORD, and let all flesh *bless his holy name* forever and ever."

Appendix 1

Charts for Further Study

As an example of what can be done with each characteristic of God, a chart could be made that summarizes each quality studied. With the following chart, I'd like to illustrate one way to look at the vastness of God's love. If you have ever faced the thought, *No one loves me*, or *Does God really love me?*, then make a chart like the one illustrated and fill it in with all the verses of the love of God found in the Bible.

One of the tools that helps us crystallize in our minds (and is also a good teaching tool) is making a chart to summarize a body of truth. Each character quality of God can be summarized separately with three or four columns. The first column would give the Scripture reference; the second would give the nugget of truth found in that verse(s) that is explained; the third would then list the action or response from us that the verse(s) point out; and finally a fourth column could list other character qualities of God that are mentioned alongside the particular one a person is studying. The following is just the beginning of a sample suggested chart.

The following chart helps us connect the character quality of God's love with our need for love. Scan down through the chart and see how God revealed His love to each individual and nation. This partial list puts in capsule form some of the thoughts gleaned about each character quality of God, and in this example, God's love.

God's Love in Action

Scripture reference	Who is loved?	Action or result
Psalm 42:8	David	God comes to me each day and night.
Psalm 89:33	David	God's kindness and love will never be taken away; His faithfulness will not fail.
Deuteronomy 10:15	Fatherless; Widow; Stranger	Give them food and clothing.
Isaiah 38:9–17	Hezekiah	Delivered his soul from the pit of corruption (death); Cast all his sins behind His back.
Psalm 103:13	Those that fear Him	The Lord pities—like a father pities his children.
Hosea 11:1	Israel	God loved when a child. God called His "son," Israel, out of Egypt.
Romans 5:8	Sinners	God demonstrates His love by loving us when we were still sinners.
2 Corinthians 9:7	Giving believers	When they give cheerfully!
Isaiah 62:4, 5	Israel	No more forsaken or desolate.
Ezekiel 34:31	Restored Israel	You are My flock—I am your God.
John 16:27	Disciples	The Father loves you because you loved Me (Jesus).
Luke 15:4–7	Lost sheep	Jesus came to save; leaves ninety-nine and goes out into the mountains and searches for that one lost sheep, and then He comes back rejoicing!

Appendix 2

List of the Character Qualities and Word Descriptions of God

Eternal	Faithful	Foreknowledge	Glory	Goodness
Grace	Guide	Holy	Immutable	Jealous
Judge/Justice	Knowledge	Longsuffering	Love	Mercy
Infinite	Power	Righteousness	Incomprehensible	Impartial
Anger	Omnipotent	Omnipresent	Perfection	Personality
Ubiquitous	Unity	Truth	Spirit	Self-existent
Person	Invisible	Access	Wisdom	Unsearchable
Creator	Providence	Savior	Works	Fatherhood
Preserver	Appearances of	Name	Repentance	Sovereign
Comforter	Light	Proclaimed Laughs	Mysterious	

(This list was compiled from many sources.)

Appendix 3

Alternate List of the Character Qualities of God

Able	Almighty	Abounding in love	All-knowing	All-powerful
Attentive	Awesome	Beautiful	Blameless	Blessed
Compassionate	Consuming fire	Enthroned	Eternal	Exalted
Faithful	First	Flawless	Forgiving	Gentle
Glorious	Good	Gracious	Has authority	Has integrity
Healing	Holy	Indescribable	Invisible	Jealous
Just	Kind	Last	Light	Living
Majestic	Merciful	Mighty	Patient	Peaceful
Perfect	Protective	Pure	Radiant	Righteous
Slow to anger	Spirit	Strong	Supreme	Sure
Tender	True	Understanding	Unfailing love	Unique
Wise	Wonderful	Worthy of praise		

(This list was compiled from many sources.)

Verses That Mention Each Character Quality of God Used in this Book

God's Love

Deuteronomy 4:37	Deuteronomy 9:29	Deuteronomy 7:7–8	Deuteronomy 33:3, 12
1 Kings 8:51–53	2 Samuel 12:24	Nehemiah 13:26	Job 7:17
Psalm 42:8	Psalm 47:4	Psalm 63:3	Psalm 78:61, 70–72
Psalm 89:32	Psalm 103:13	Psalm 146:8	Proverbs 15:9
Isaiah 38:17	Isaiah 43:4	Jeremiah 31:3	Hosea 11:1
Malachi 1:2	John 3:16	John 5:20	John 14:21, 23, 24
John 16:27	John 17:10, 23, 26	John 20:17	Romans 1:17
Romans 5:8	Romans 9:13	Romans 11:28	2 Corinthians 9:7
2 Corinthians 13:11, 14	Ephesians 2:4–5	2 Thessalonians 2:16	Titus 3:4–5
Hebrews 12:6	1 John 3:4	1 John 4:5, 7, 9–10	1 John 4:12–16, 19
Jude 21	Revelation 3:12	Revelation 14:1	

Examples of God's Love

Genesis 46:3	Genesis 17:7	Exodus 3:6	Exodus 29:45–46
Exodus 19:4–6	Leviticus 20:24, 26	Leviticus 22:32–33	Leviticus 11:44–45
Leviticus 25:38	Numbers 15:41	Leviticus 25:23, 42, 55	Leviticus 26:12
Deuteronomy 4:20, 34, 37	Deuteronomy 9:29	1 Kings 8:51–53	Deuteronomy 7:6–8, 13
Deuteronomy 10:15	Deuteronomy 14:2	Deuteronomy 23:5	Deuteronomy 26:18–19
Deuteronomy 27:9	Deuteronomy 28:9–10	Deuteronomy 32:9–12	Deuteronomy 33:3, 12
2 Samuel 7:23–24	1 Samuel 12:24	Psalm 4:3	Psalm 31:19–21
Psalm 42:8	Psalm 47:4	Psalm 48:9, 14	Psalm 50:5, 7
Psalm 63:3	Psalm 73:1	Psalm 74:2	Psalm 78:61–62
Psalm 81:13	Psalm 89:33	Psalm 90:1	Psalm 100:3
Psalm 79:13	Psalm 95:7	Psalm 103:4	Psalm 105:6
Psalm 114:2	Psalm 135:4	Psalm 148:14	Proverbs 11:20
Proverbs 15:9	Isaiah 5:7	Isaiah 41:8–10	Isaiah 43:1–5, 7
Isaiah 44:1–2, 21, 23	Isaiah 48:12	Isaiah 49:13–17	Isaiah 51:16
Isaiah 54:5–10	Isaiah 62:4–5	Isaiah 64:4	Isaiah 65:19
Isaiah 66:13	Jeremiah 3:14–15	Jeremiah 10:16	Jeremiah 51:19
Jeremiah 12:7	Jeremiah 13:11	Jeremiah 15:16	Jeremiah 31:3, 14, 32
Jeremiah 32:41	Ezekiel 16:8	Ezekiel 34:31	Ezekiel 37:27
Hosea 2:19–20, 23	Hosea 9:10	Hosea 11:1, 3–4	Zephaniah 3:17
Haggai 2:23	Zechariah 1:14	Zechariah 2:8	Zechariah 8:8

Jeremiah 30:22	Zechariah 13:9	Malachi 2:23	Malachi 3:16–17
Matthew 18:11–14	Luke 15:4–7, 11–27	I Peter 2:10	John 14:21, 23
John 16:27	John 17:10, 26	Romans 1:7	Romans 5:8
Romans 8:31–39	Romans 11:28	1Corinthians 2:9	1 Corinthians 3:9
1 Corinthians 7:23	1 Corinthians 6:19–20	2 Corinthians 5:18–21	2 Corinthians 6:16
2 Corinthians 13:14	Colossians 3:12	Hebrews 11:16	Ephesians 1:3–6
1 Thessalonians 1:4	James 1:18		

Power

Exodus 15:3, 6–8, 10–12	Numbers 11:23	Numbers 23:20	Deuteronomy 3:24
Deuteronomy 7:21	Deuteronomy 11:2	Deuteronomy 32:39	Job 10:7
Deuteronomy 33:26–27	Joshua 4:24	1 Samuel 2:6–10	1 Samuel 14:6
1 Samuel 14:6	2 Samuel 22:13	1 Chronicles 29:11–12	2 Chronicles 14:11
2 Chronicles 16:9	2 Chronicles 20:6	Psalm 103:17	2 Chronicles 25:8–9
Ezra 8:22	Nehemiah 1:10	Job 9:4–5, 10–13, 19	Job 5:9
Job 11:10	Job 12:14–16	Job 14:20	Job 23:13–14
Job 26:11–12, 14	Job 34:14–15	Job 36:5, 22, 27–33	Job 37:1–23
Job 38:8, 37	Job 40:9	Job 41:10	Job 42:2
Psalm 18	Psalm 2:3–5	Psalm 21:13	Psalm 29:3–11
Psalm 33:9	Psalm 46:1, 6	Psalm 62:11	Psalm 65:6–7
Psalm 66:3, 7	Psalm 68:33–35	Psalm 74:13–15	Psalm 76:6–7
Psalm 77:14, 16, 18	Psalm 78:12–16, 26, 43–51	Psalm 79:11	Psalm 89:8–10, 13
Psalm 90:3, 11	Psalm 97:3–5	Psalm 104:7, 9, 29–30, 32	Psalm 105

Psalm 114:3–8	Psalm 135:8–12	Psalm 136:10–22	Psalm 106:8
Psalm 107:25, 29	Psalm 111:6	Psalm 114:3–8	Psalm 115:3
Psalm 118:16	Psalm 135:6	Psalm 144:5–6	Psalm 145:6, 11–12
Psalm 136:10–22	Psalm 147:5, 16, 18	Psalm 148:5, 8	Proverbs 21:30
Proverbs 30:4	Isaiah 14:24, 27	Isaiah 17:13	Isaiah 19:11
Isaiah 23:11	Isaiah 26:4	Isaiah 27:4	Isaiah 31:3
Isaiah 33:3, 13	Isaiah 40:12, 22, 24, 26, 28	Isaiah 43:13, 16, 17	Isaiah 44:2, 7
Isaiah 46:10–11	Isaiah 48:13	Isaiah 50:2, 3	Isaiah 51:10, 15
Isaiah 52:10	Isaiah 59:1	Isaiah 60:16	Isaiah 63:12
Jeremiah 5:22	Jeremiah 10:6, 12–13	Jeremiah 51:15	Jeremiah 20:11
Jeremiah 27:5	Jeremiah 32:17, 27	Jeremiah 50:44	Daniel 2:20–22
Daniel 3:17	Daniel 6:27	Joel 2:11	Joel 3:16
Amos 4:13	Amos 9:5–6	Micah 1:3–4	Nahum 1:3–6
Habakkuk 3:6, 9–11, 15	Zechariah 9:14	Matthew 3:19	Matthew 6:13
Matthew 10:28	Matthew 19:26	Matthew 22:29	Mark 14:36
Luke 1:37, 49, 51	Luke 11:20	Romans 1:20	Romans 4:21
1 Corinthians 6:14	2 Corinthians 13:4	Ephesians 1:19–20	Ephesians 3:20–21
Hebrews 1:3	Hebrews 12:26–29	James 4:12	1 Peter 1:5
Revelation 4:11	Revelation 11:17	Revelation 19:1, 6	

Truth

Numbers 23:19	Deuteronomy 32:4	1 Samuel 15:29	Psalm 25:10
Psalm 31:5	Psalm 33:4	Psalm 40:10	Psalm 43:3

Psalm 57:3 Psalm 71:22 Psalm 86:11,15 Psalm 91:4

Psalm 100:5 Psalm 117:2 Psalm 108:4 Psalm 132:11

Psalm 138:2 Psalm 146:6 Isaiah 25:1 Isaiah 65:16

Jeremiah 10:10 Daniel 4:37 Daniel 9:13 John 8:26

John 17:17 Romans 3:4, 7 Titus 1:2 Revelation 6:10

Revelation 15:3 1 Timothy 3:15 John 18:38 Psalm 119:160

Proverbs 30:5

Judge/Judgment

Genesis 16:5	Genesis 18:20–21, 25	Numbers 16:22	Deuteronomy 10:17
Deuteronomy 32:3–5	Joshua 24:19	Exodus 20:5	Exodus 34:7
Judges 11:27	1 Samuel 2:3, 10	1 Samuel 24:12–13	2 Samuel 14:14
2 Samuel 22:25–27	1 Kings 8:32	Judges 9:56–57	2 Chronicles 6:22–23
2 Chronicles 19:6–7	1 Chronicles 16:33	Nehemiah 9:33	Job 4:17
Job 8:3	Job 9:15, 28	Job 23:7	Job 31:13–15
Psalm 18:25–26	Job 34:10–12, 17, 19, 23	Job 35:14	Job 36:3,19
Job 37:23	Psalm 7:8–9, 11	Psalm 9:4, 7–9, 16	Psalm 11:4–7
Psalm 19:9	Psalm 26:1–2	Psalm 33:5	Psalm 35:24
Psalm 43:1	Psalm 50:4, 6	Psalm 75:7	Psalm 51:4
Psalm 58:11	Psalm 62:12	Psalm 67:4	Psalm 71:19
Psalm 76:8–9	Psalm 85:10	Psalm 89:14	Psalm 90:8, 11
Psalm 92:15	Psalm 94:1–2, 10	Psalm 82:1–4, 8	Psalm 96:10, 13
Psalm 97:2	Psalm 98:9	Psalm 99:4, 8	Psalm 103:6

Psalm 111:7	Psalm 119:37	Psalm 129:4	Psalm 135:14
Psalm 143:2	Psalm 145:17	Proverbs 11:31	Proverbs 16:2
Proverbs 17:3	Proverbs 21:2–3	Proverbs 24:11–12	Proverbs 29:13, 26
Ecclesiastes 3:15, 17	Ecclesiastes 11:7	Ecclesiastes 12:14	Isaiah 1:27
Isaiah 3:13–14	Isaiah 10:17–18	Isaiah 26:7–9	Isaiah 30:18, 27, 30
Isaiah 31:2	Isaiah 33:22	Isaiah 45:21	Isaiah 61:8
Jeremiah 9:24	Jeremiah 10:10	Jeremiah 11:20	Jeremiah 20:12
Jeremiah 12:1	Jeremiah 32:19	Jeremiah 50:7	Jeremiah 51:10
Lamentations 1:18	Ezekiel 14:23	Ezekiel 18:25, 29–30	Ezekiel 33:7–20
Daniel 7:9–10	Daniel 4:24, 37	Daniel 9:7.14	Hosea 10:10
Amos 8:7	Amos 10:34–35	Romans 1:32	Romans 2:2–16
Romans 3:4–6, 26	Romans 9:14	Romans 11:22	Ephesians 6:8–9
Colossians 3:25	2 Thessalonians 1:4–6	Hebrews 6:10	Hebrews 10:30–31
Hebrews 12:22–23, 29	1 Peter 1:17	2 Peter 2:9	1 John 1:1, 9
Jude 6	Revelation 6:16–17	Revelation 11:18	Revelation 15:3–4, 13
Revelation 16:5–7	Revelation 18:8	Revelation 19:2	

Access

Deuteronomy 4:7	Psalm 24:3–4	Psalm 27:4	Psalm 43:3
Psalm 65:4	Psalm 145:18	Isaiah 55:3	Matthew 6:6
John 10:7, 9	John 14:6	Acts 14:27	Romans 5:2
Ephesians 2:13	Ephesians 3:12	Colossians 2:21–22	Hebrews 4:16
Hebrews 7:19–25	Hebrews 10:19–22	Hebrews 11:6	James 4:8
1 Peter 1:17	1 Peter 3:18	1 John 4:16	Hebrews 6:19–20
Psalm 68:5			

Presence

Genesis 16:13	Genesis 28:16	Exodus 20:24	Deuteronomy 4:34–36, 39
Joshua 2:11	1 Kings 8:27	2 Chronicles 2:6	Psalm 139:3, 5–12
Isaiah 57:15	Isaiah 66:1	Jeremiah 23:23–24	Jeremiah 32:18–19
Jonah 1:3–4	Acts 7:48–49	Acts 17:24, 27–28	1 Chronicles 12:6
Ephesians 1:23			

Righteousness

Judges 5:11	Ezra 9:15	Job 36:3	Psalm 5:8
Psalm 7:9	Psalm 48:10	Psalm 50:6	Psalm 71:15, 19
Psalm 72:1	Psalm 88:12	Psalm 89:16	Psalm 82:14
Psalm 97:2	Psalm 111:3	Psalm 116:5	Psalm 119:40, 137, 142, 144, 172
Psalm 9:4, 8	Psalm 143:1	Psalm 145:7, 17	Isaiah 41:10
Psalm 51:1–8	Isaiah 56:1	Isaiah 46:12–13	Jeremiah 4:2
Jeremiah 9:24, 30–32	Jeremiah 12:1	Lamentations 3:34–36	Daniel 9:7, 14
Hosea 14:9	Micah 7:9	Matthew 6:32	John 17:25
Acts 17:30–31	Romans 1:17	Romans 3:4–6, 21–22, 25–26	Romans 9:14
Romans 10:3–4	2 Timothy 4:8	1 Peter 2:23	2 Peter 1:1
1 John 2:1	Revelation 16:5	Psalm 11:7	

Wisdom

Ezra 7:25	Job 9:4	Job 12:13, 16	Psalm 104:24
Psalm 136:5	Psalm 147:5	Proverbs 3:19–20	Proverbs 8:12, 22, 27–31
Isaiah 31:2	Jeremiah 10:7, 12	Jeremiah 51:15	Daniel 2:20–22, 28
Romans 16:27	1 Corinthians 1:24–25	Ephesians 3:10	1 Timothy 1:17
Revelation 7:12			

Incomprehensible

Exodus 20:21	Deuteronomy 4:11	Deuteronomy 5:22–27	1 Kings 8:12
Job 11:7–9	Job 15:8	Job 37:1–24	Psalm 18:11
Psalm 97:2	Ecclesiastes 3:11	Isaiah 40:12–31	Isaiah 55:8–9
1 Corinthians 2:16			

Holy

Exodus 3:5	Exodus 15:11, 13	Leviticus 19:2	Leviticus 11:44–45
Leviticus 21:6–8	Deuteronomy 32:4	Joshua 5:15	Joshua 24:19
1 Samuel 2:2	1 Samuel 6:20	1 Chronicles 16:10	Job 4:17–19
Job 6:10	Job 15:15	Job 25:5	Job 34:20
Job 36:23	Psalm 105:3	Psalm 11:4, 7	Psalm 18:30
Psalm 22:3	Psalm 30:4	Psalm 33:4–5	Psalm 36:6
Psalm 37:8	Psalm 48:1, 10	Psalm 60:6	Psalm 89:35
Psalm 108:7	Psalm 92:15	Psalm 99:3, 5, 9	Psalm 111:9
Psalm 119:142	Psalm 145:17	Proverbs 9:10	Isaiah 5:16
Isaiah 6:3	Isaiah 12:6	Isaiah 41:14, 16, 21	Isaiah 43:3, 14–15

Isaiah 45:19	Isaiah 47:4	Isaiah 49:7	Isaiah 52:10
Isaiah 57:15	Jeremiah 2:5	Lamentations 3:38	Ezekiel 39:7, 25
Ezekiel 36:21–22	Daniel 4:8–9	Habakkuk 1:12–13	Matthew 5:48
Matthew 19:17	Mark 10:18	Luke 18:19	Luke 1:49
John 7:28	John 17:11	Romans 1:23	Hebrews 1:8
James 1:13	1 Peter 1:15–16	1 John 1:5	1 John 2:20
Revelation 4:8	Revelation 15:4		

Epilogue

For years people have wanted to know about our mysterious God. We want to understand who He is, what He is like, and more. And guess what? God has revealed Himself in His Word! We can learn more about Him if we look closely enough.

In *God: Know Seek Worship*, readers will take a journey through the Bible with author David B. Virts, looking at the many word descriptions God gave man. Man can learn much about God from nature, but what we can discover there cannot compare to what can be discovered by a close study of God's Word, where He has left us incredible word pictures of Himself. Through His Word we can get to know the character of God. And in this book readers will delve into the word pictures to gain understanding of each character quality and begin to see and seek God like never before. With this knowledge your relationship with God will grow deeper, and you'll worship God with new zeal. Soon you'll understand our true purpose—to forever reflect God's mercy, love, and forgiveness.

Don't miss this amazing opportunity to get to know God. There is so much to uncover!

David B. Virts has made a lifelong study of the Scriptures, starting with graduating from Prairie Bible Institute and taking further studies at Grace College of the Bible. For the last twenty years, he has spent twenty to thirty hours a week reading, studying, memorizing, and meditating on the Word. He began teaching Sunday school forty years ago and has been active in various church work and ministries. He has developed a curriculum for new Christians called FoundationStones and has been heavily involved as a layman. He has written more than sixteen hundred devotionals that were printed weekly in the *Rutherford Reader* (www.rutherfordreader.com) for 6 years and heard daily over WNAH, 1360 AM in Nashville, Tennessee. He now lives in the Tennessee and Alabama area with his wife Shirley and near his daughter Katrina.